HOW TO HONG KONG

by Lena Sin & Nicholas Tay

How to Hong Kong

ISBN 978-988-13765-7-2

First printing 2017

Published by Blacksmith Books
Unit 26, 19/F, Block B, Wah Lok Industrial Centre,
37-41 Shan Mei St, Fo Tan, Hong Kong
Tel: (+852) 2877 7899 • www.blacksmithbooks.com

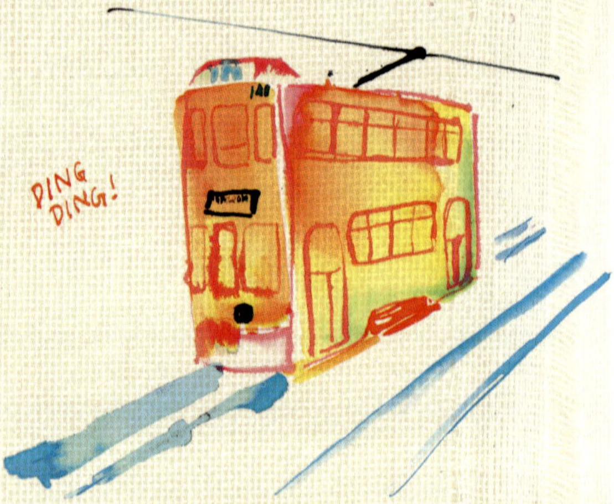

Contents

香港

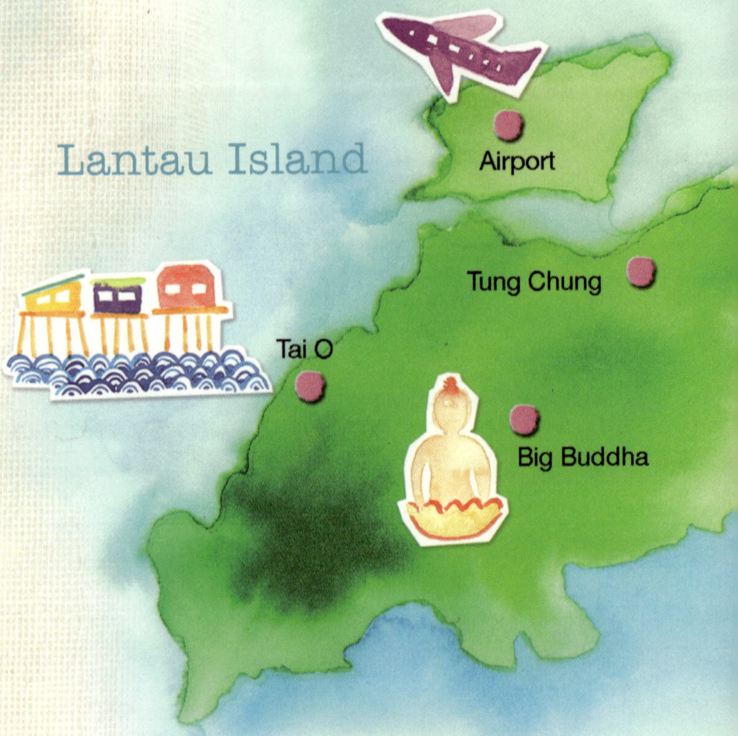

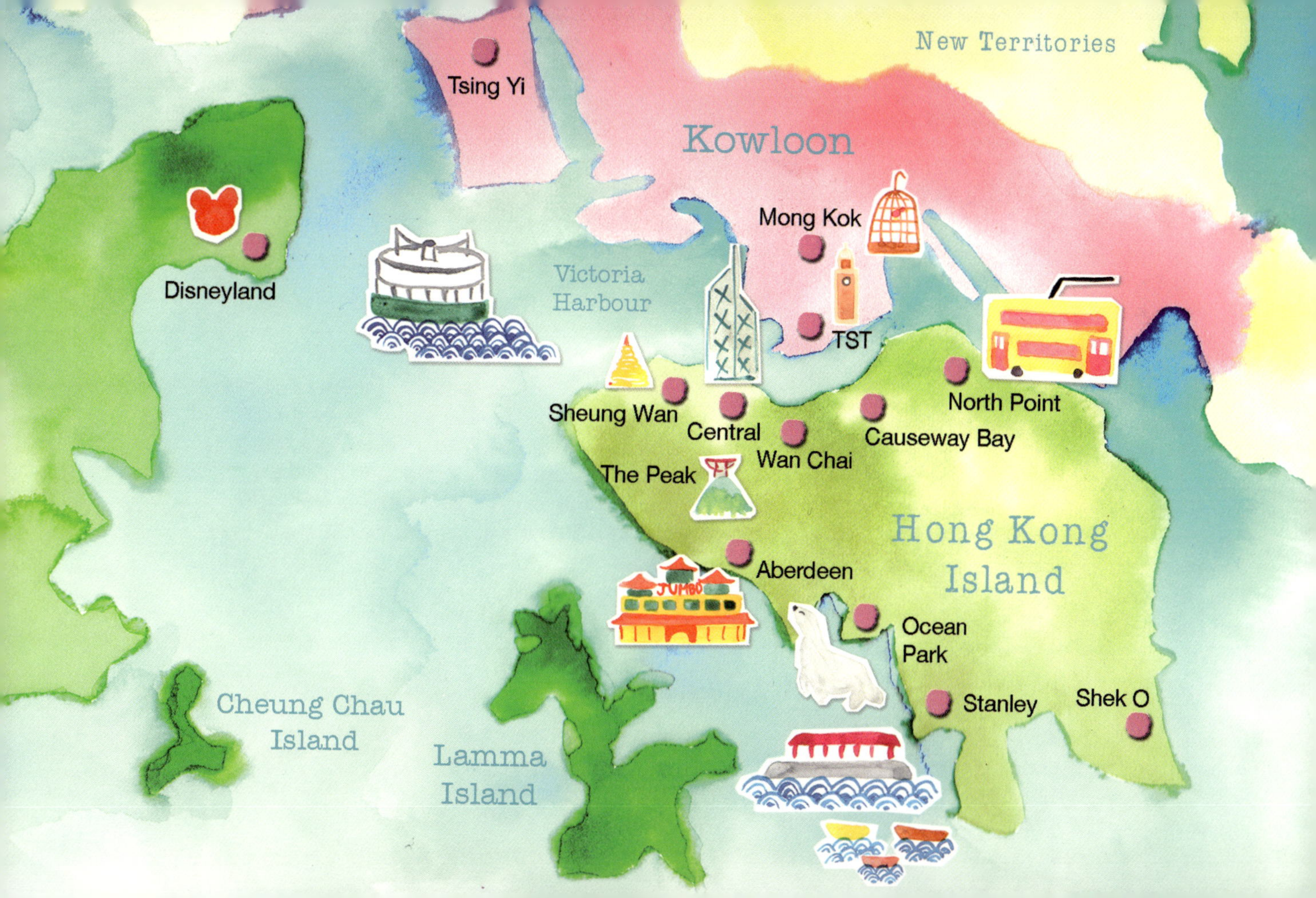
New Territories
Tsing Yi
Kowloon
Mong Kok
Disneyland
Victoria Harbour
TST
North Point
Sheung Wan
Central
Wan Chai
Causeway Bay
The Peak
Hong Kong Island
Aberdeen
JUMBO
Ocean Park
Stanley
Shek O
Cheung Chau Island
Lamma Island

Introduction

"Moth balls and the smell of sewage! We're home!" the boy exclaimed, foppish brown hair cresting the top of his eyes. He looked up at his father, who only nodded and smiled. And so did I.

It was such an apt declaration of love. The look of glee on his face and air of excitement knowing that we were, finally, speeding headlong in a train to the main airport terminal, through ultra-efficient customs, baggage collection, and then into that blast of steamy night-time air that always signals 'home.' I knew exactly how he felt.

Some places are so beautiful they need no introduction: The golden hills of Tuscany, the swaying rice fields of Bali. Hong Kong is not one of them, despite her fabled charm. There are days when the mayhem, the crash and zeal of skyscrapers and people become too much. For this is a place that challenges you to peel back the layers, to wade into her mysteries and contradictions to see the humanity in a city that is often stretched to the edge. For those of us who've had the good fortune to know and love her, the feeling is akin to how a parent feels about their child: still the best thing to ever happen, moth balls and sewage and all.

I was born in Hong Kong and more or less raised here, save for a few early years in Canada. When I was seven, we moved here for good, trading snow forts for hot, sticky summers. It was an easy transition, an arrow straight to the heart; this was always home. My childhood of the late '80s was sprinkled with secret joys: It will forever be the No. 22 minibus, tracing that familiar journey from Star Ferry to Pokfulam, shimmering water views chasing us all the way home. It's junk trips and the smell of gasoline and salt water, throwing myself into the ocean while my brother weighed the likelihood of sharks lurking in the South China Sea. It's ninth birthday parties on a tram, rattling our way through the city, and cheap thrills in a pool during a Typhoon 1, bobbing in a makeshift wave pool before getting kicked out by life guards.

Hong Kong will always be about these hidden moments; anyone who's ever loved this city has their own version. A pastiche of a million untold stories to make up something intangible that many simply refer to as the 'energy' of this city. A layered mash-up of humid nights on the town, quiet hillside treks, noisy restaurant gatherings, crowded throngs of shoppers, washing hanging out of cluttered windows, the smell of dried seafood and incense wafting from doorsteps into the sky. For all its brashness, Hong Kong is also an improbably intimate place.

And while I no longer live here, she continues to romance me, pulling me back every year with her kinetic charm. I've enjoyed many seasons here, both as tour guide and tourist, showing my husband old haunts while discovering new ones. Looking back, it was probably our first trip together in the fall of 2007 that formed the beginning of this book. Newly married, Nick and I came to Hong Kong for our second wedding banquet. Seeing him, and a few of our friends who joined us on the trip, discover the city for the first time helped me fall in love all over again. We've chronicled some of those moments here. Much of what I write about takes place between 2007 and now, but this is also a timeless journey. Hong Kong may be continually charged up and ready to chase her future, but that indefinable quality of aliveness remains threaded through and through no matter the era.

So here we go: Notebook, camera and sketchbook in hand. Our voracious appetite for this city and her stories. If travel is about the singular joy of discovery, we hope you find some of that here. I've come to believe wonder can be found no matter where you are, but when the sensation has dulled, there is nothing like travel to jolt you back to life. Especially, for us, if the destination happens to be home.

Lena Sin

Go Slow in

SHEUNG WAN

Searching for Old Hong Kong

If nostalgia is hereditary, then mine must come from my mother who's prone to reminding me time and again how much better the Hong Kong of her childhood was — a time when the streets felt wide and breezy, the city more a village than a metropolis. It was one of poverty, too, no doubt for most Hong Kongers, but that seemed to matter less. "Everyone was the same," she'd tell me in Cantonese. "You didn't feel poor."

She misses that time.

I share my mother's devotion to that picture of simplicity, though I've never lived it. My mother was born in 1951, and I a good 29 years later. But I've seen countless pictures and heard tales of this mythical Hong Kong: Black-and-white images of ladies in elegant *cheongsams*, rickshaws clattering their way past low-rise buildings outfitted with Hong Kong's famous street signs. A harbour dotted with red sail junks and lush hillsides dominating the backdrop.

Pretty, old colonial Hong Kong no longer exists but here in Sheung Wan, I can almost feel her spirit still lingering on. Something about the noodle-thin streets, the pungent smell of herbal shops and the way the light hits. Oh, the light.

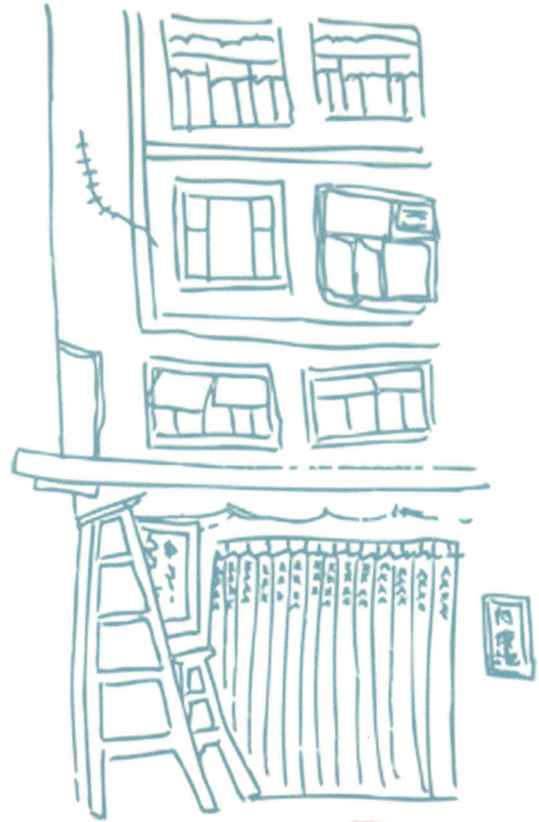

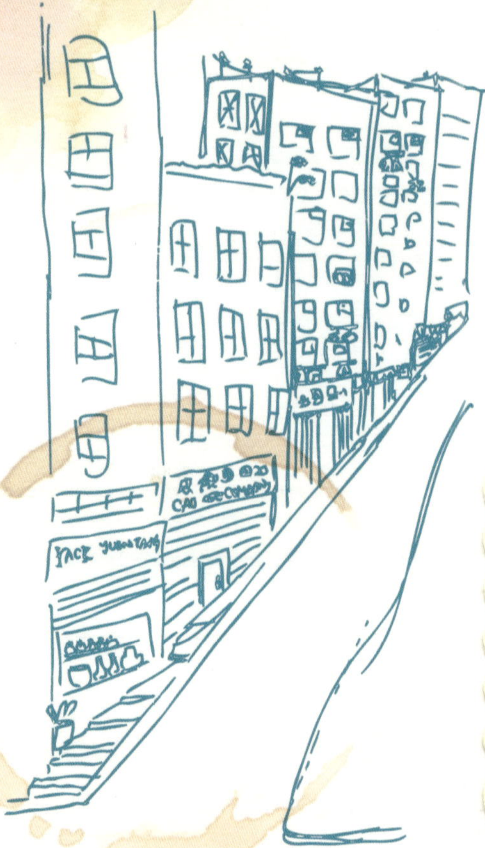

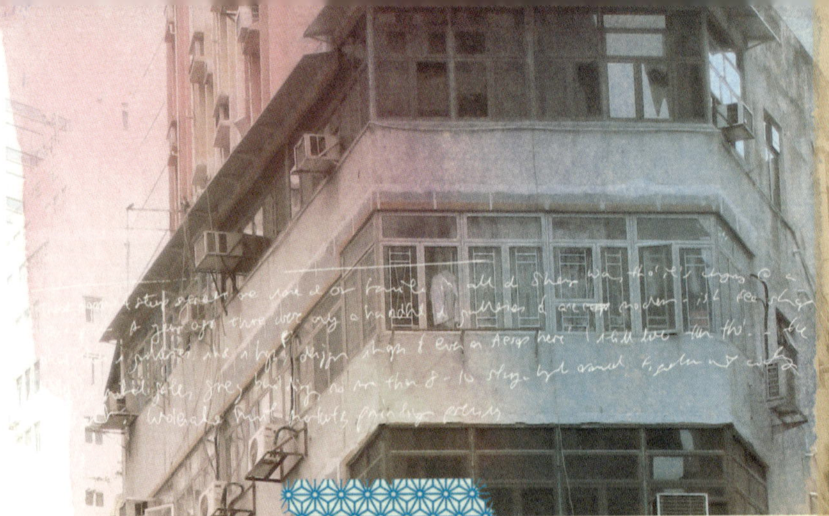

When the sun casts a hazy, afternoon glow on dusty, time-worn buildings, it's romance delivered with a dose of grunge, which to me is the landscape of Hong Kong. It's the way the afterglow shines on a tired man smoking on the steps of a steep lane, the way an invisible alley is lit so you see the welder bent over working into twilight. Life has never been easy in this town, but when you stop to look, it sure is beautiful.

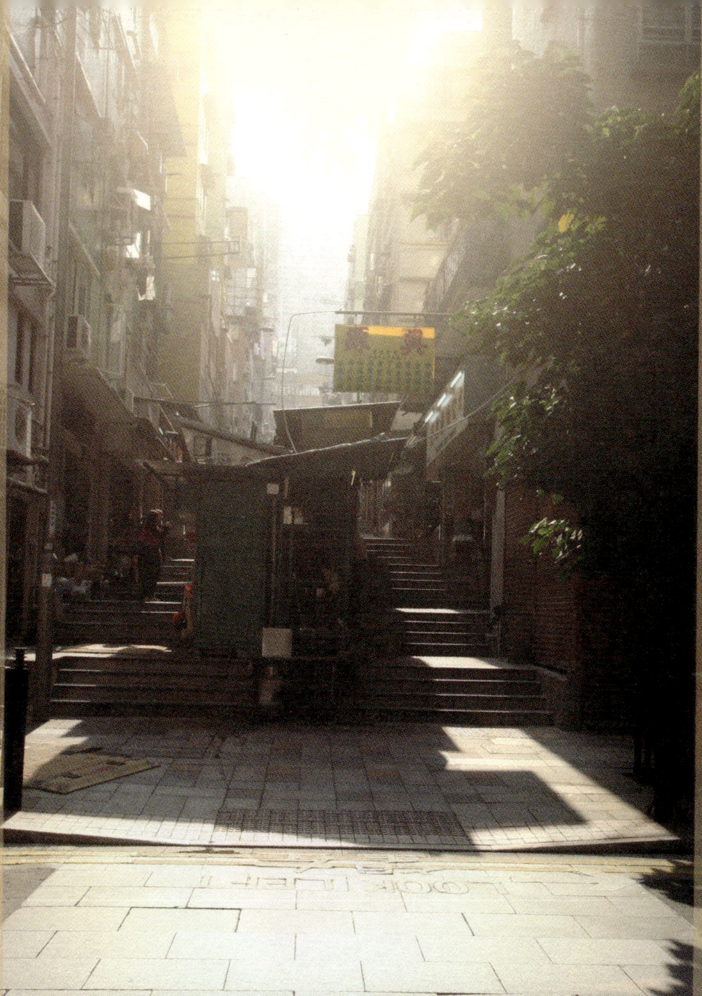

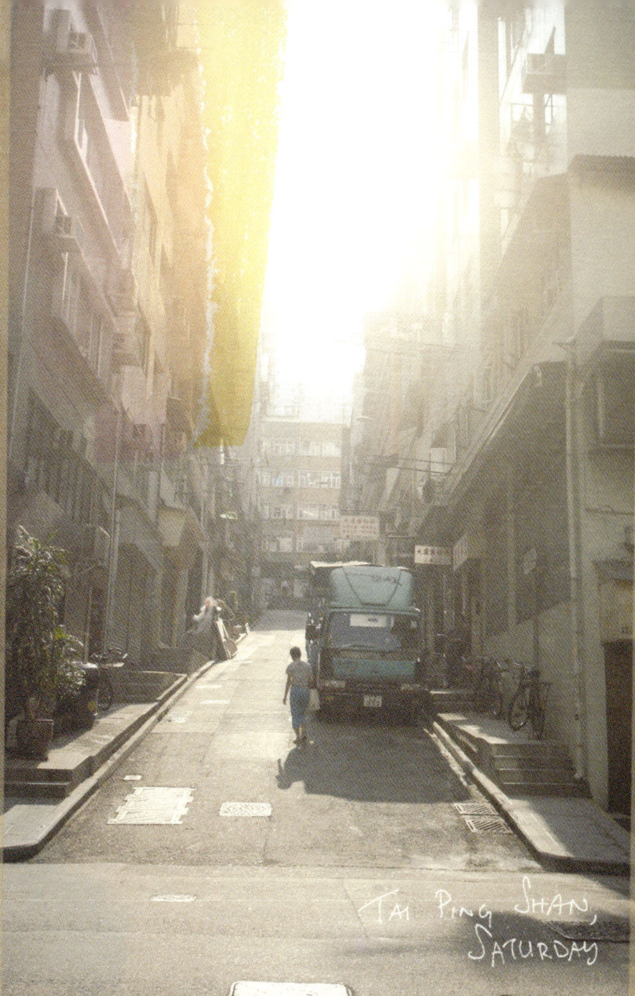

Tai Ping Shan,
Saturday

A Summer on Hollywood Road

My first official writing assignment was to review a beach. Not a movie, a book or even a restaurant, but a beach! It seemed like a hedonist's dream, this idea of lazing under the sun all in the name of *research*.

Except it was the summer of 2000 and I was a 19-year-old university student trying to exude a cool airiness about the whole affair while really feeling quite nervous. For one, I'd never written an article. And two, how much can one say about a beach beyond water quality and sand texture? Well, this is what I discovered:

"Everything about Discovery Bay screams country-club yuppiness. There's no litter on this perfectly groomed beach, it comes complete with a brick paved promenade, and even has tall luscious trees strategically planted to improve the aesthetic quality of the setting. The attire favoured here are Keds, khakis, and polo tees. Beyond the beach, you will find perfect pale yellow terraced houses — nuclear family included."

I tried to adopt the weekly's quirky, smart aleck tone. It was, admittedly, not the most brilliant piece of writing, but maybe it was better than what the editors were expecting from a lowly intern. "It's good," said the associate editor, who loomed large in my mind with her Cambridge degree and English wit. I lurched with relief and excitement. And so it was: a beach bum's guide became my first published work.

That simmering summer working on Hollywood Road turned out to be one of the best. It wasn't just discovering a vocation that I thought I could be reasonably good at. It was also the joys of gallivanting around the city, asking nosy questions of the people I found so endlessly interesting. How much does a *dai pai dong* (street food) vendor make, and what about those nasty cockroaches — are they a problem in the open-air kitchen? (Turns out, yes.) How did the Star Ferry deckhand get his job? And did you hear about those late-night paint parties tucked away in a quiet corner of Sheung Wan? After hours, I danced with my girlfriends into the night, drunk on cheap rum and giddy on possibility. On the cusp of adulthood with a licence to navigate all the hidden corners of this dizzying city, I was enthralled as ever.

Hong Kong still captivates me today, even if the version I love most will always be the one of the '90s I grew up in and the early 2000s I spent many a summer break home from university. Rediscovering it as a proper grown-up, married and all, has brought its own new perspective. I'm more aware of her flaws, less over-zealous about her virtues. Blind enchantment exchanged for a wider lens. But one thing remains the same: Hong Kong keeps shifting and shaping, inventing and reinventing – which means discovery, even without the curious wonder of youth, endures.

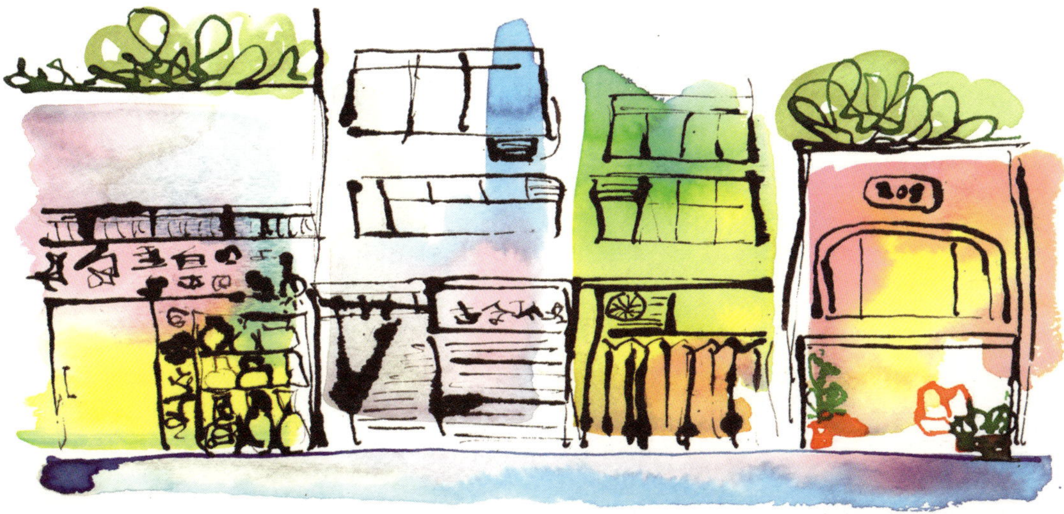

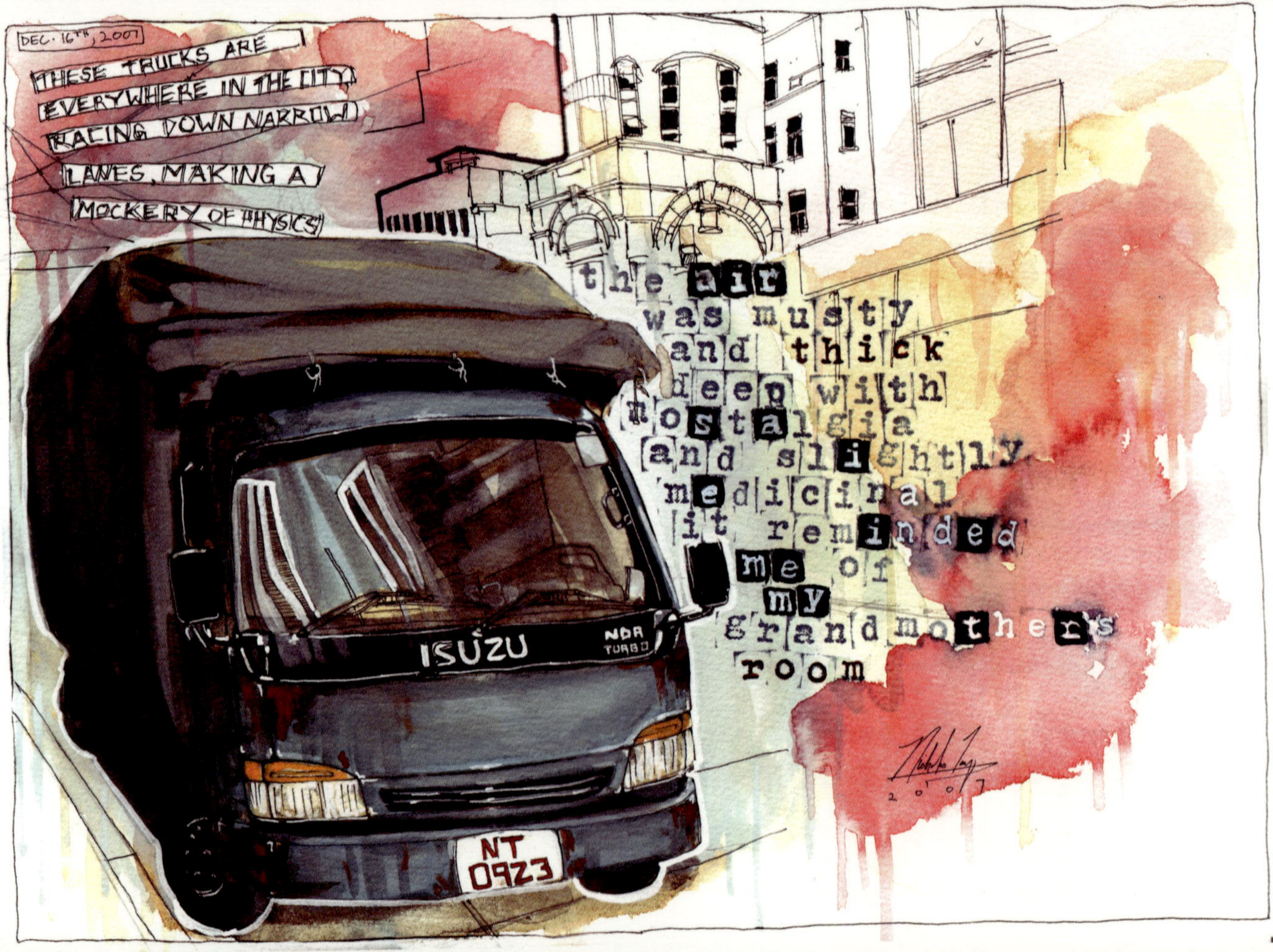
DEC. 16TH, 2007
THESE TRUCKS ARE
EVERYWHERE IN THE CITY
RACING DOWN NARROW
LANES, MAKING A
MOCKERY OF PHYSICS
the air
was musty
and thick
deep with
nostalgia
and slightly
medicinal
it reminded
me of
my
grandmothers
room
ISUZU
NDR TURBO
NT 0923
2007

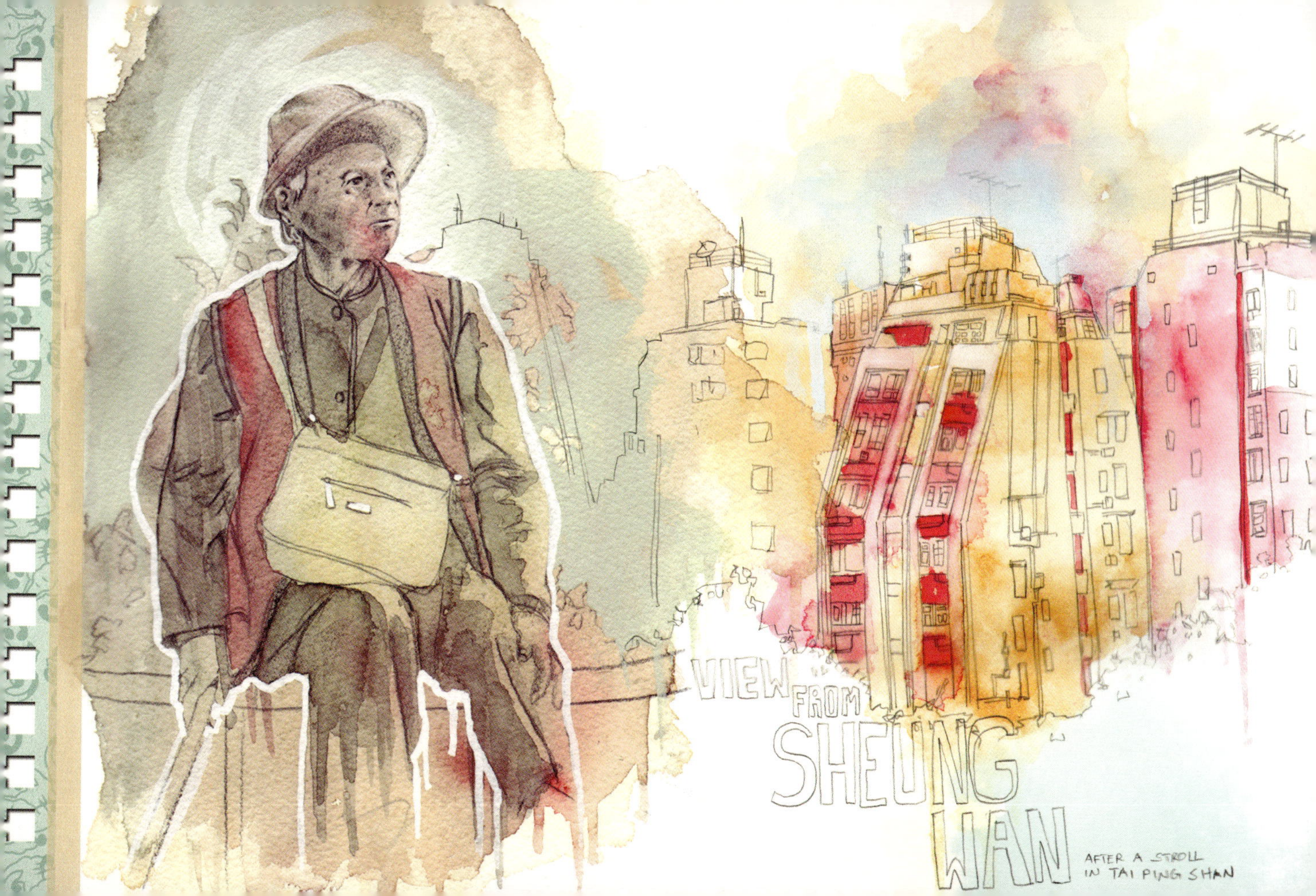
VIEW FROM SHEUNG WAN
AFTER A STROLL
IN TAI PING SHAN

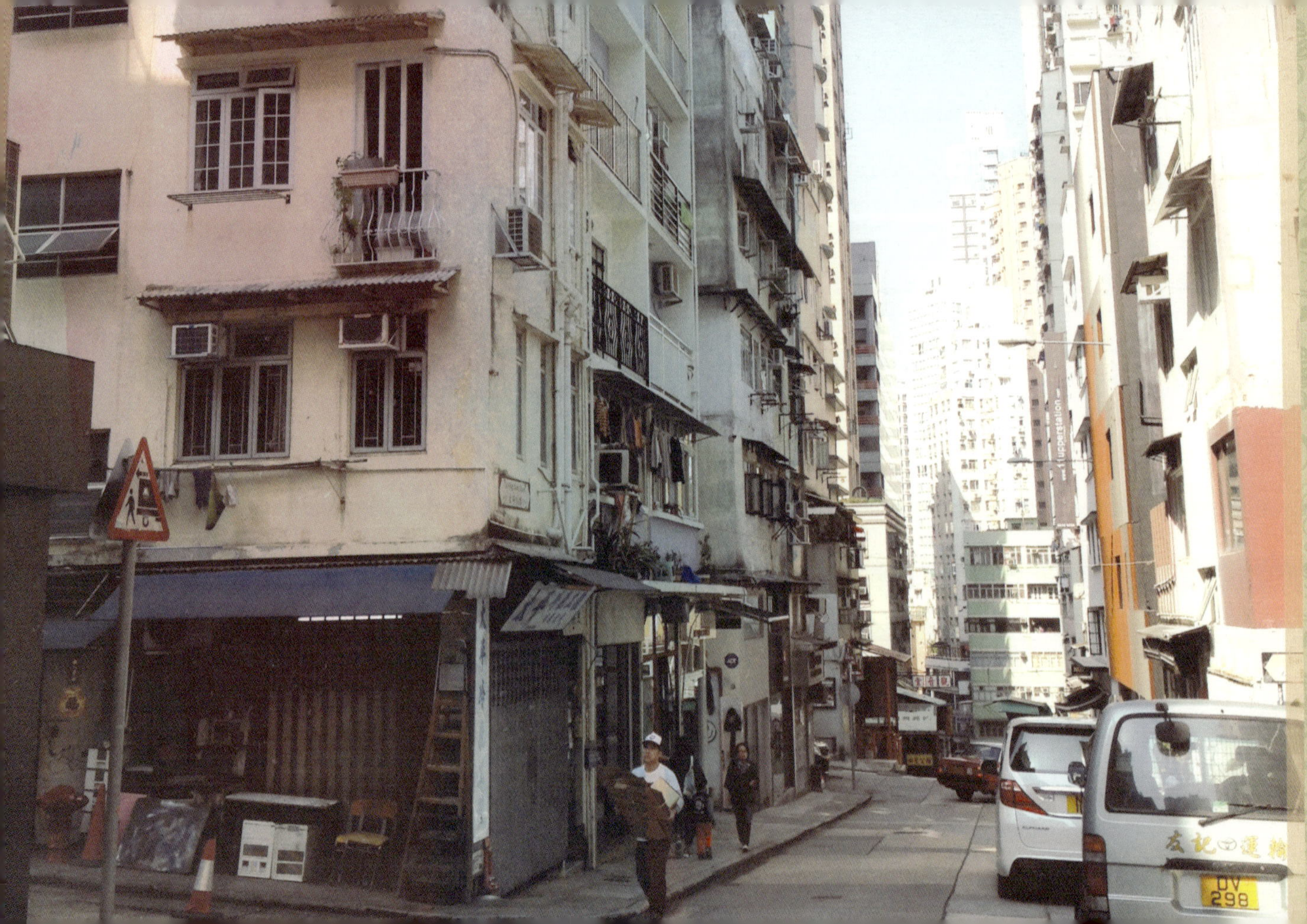
友記 運輸
DV 298

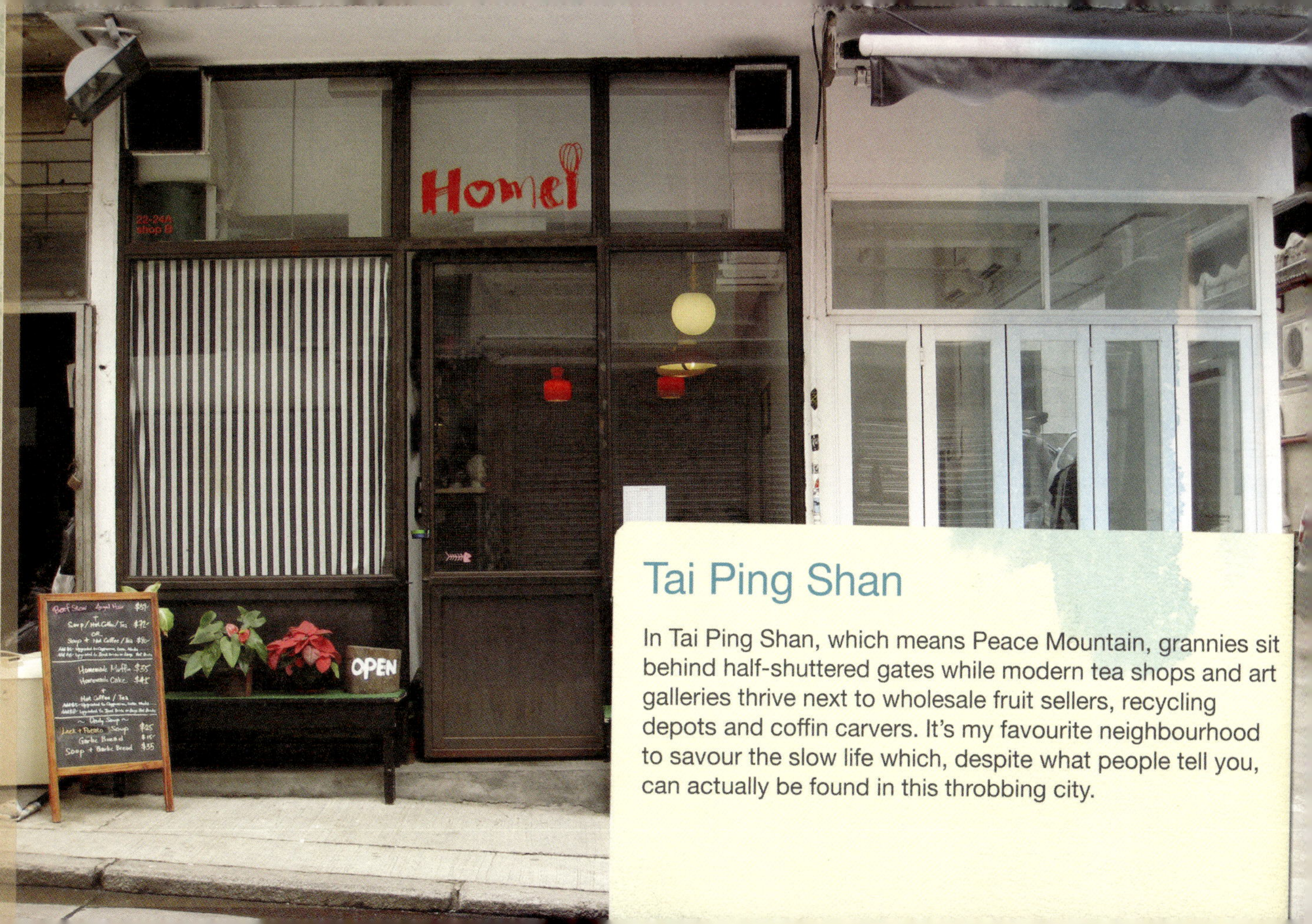

Tai Ping Shan

In Tai Ping Shan, which means Peace Mountain, grannies sit behind half-shuttered gates while modern tea shops and art galleries thrive next to wholesale fruit sellers, recycling depots and coffin carvers. It's my favourite neighbourhood to savour the slow life which, despite what people tell you, can actually be found in this throbbing city.

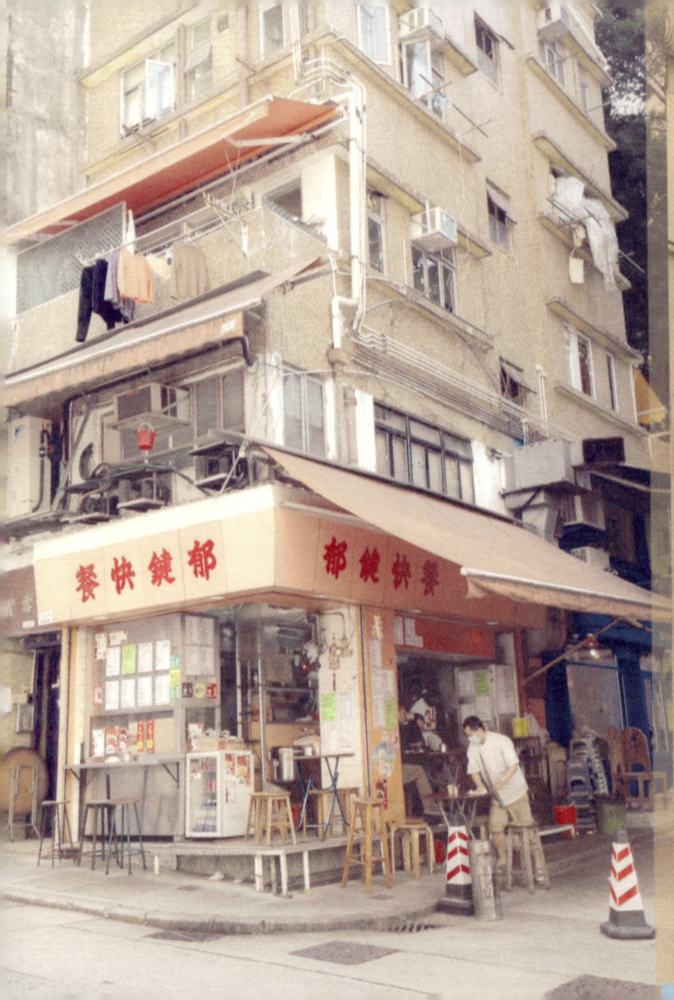
郁鍵快餐
郁鍵快餐

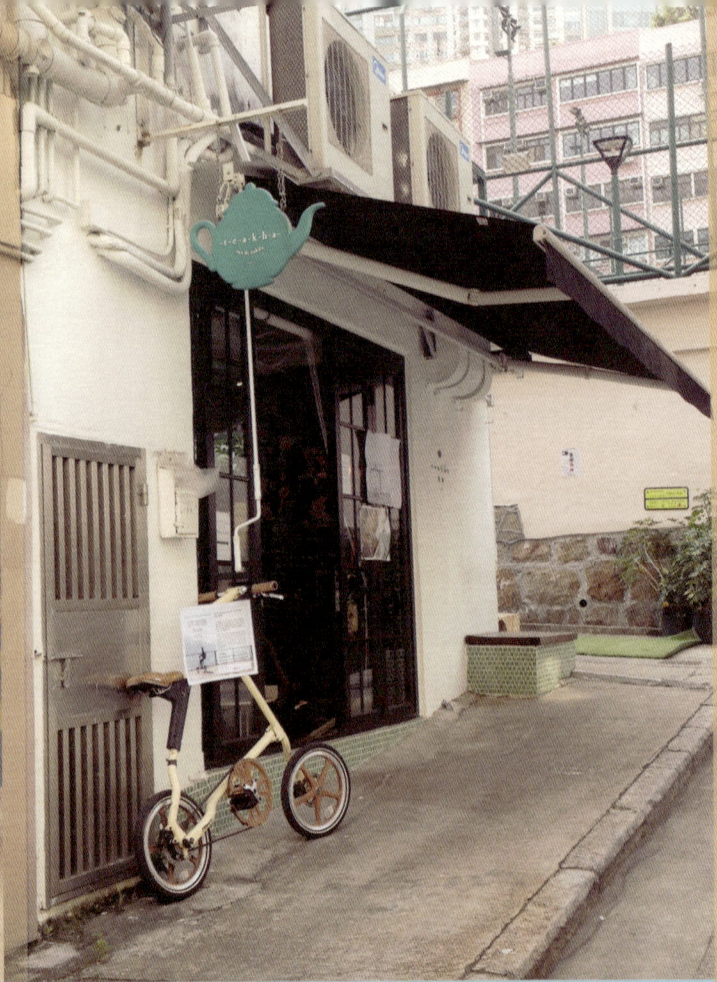
t-e-a-k-h-a

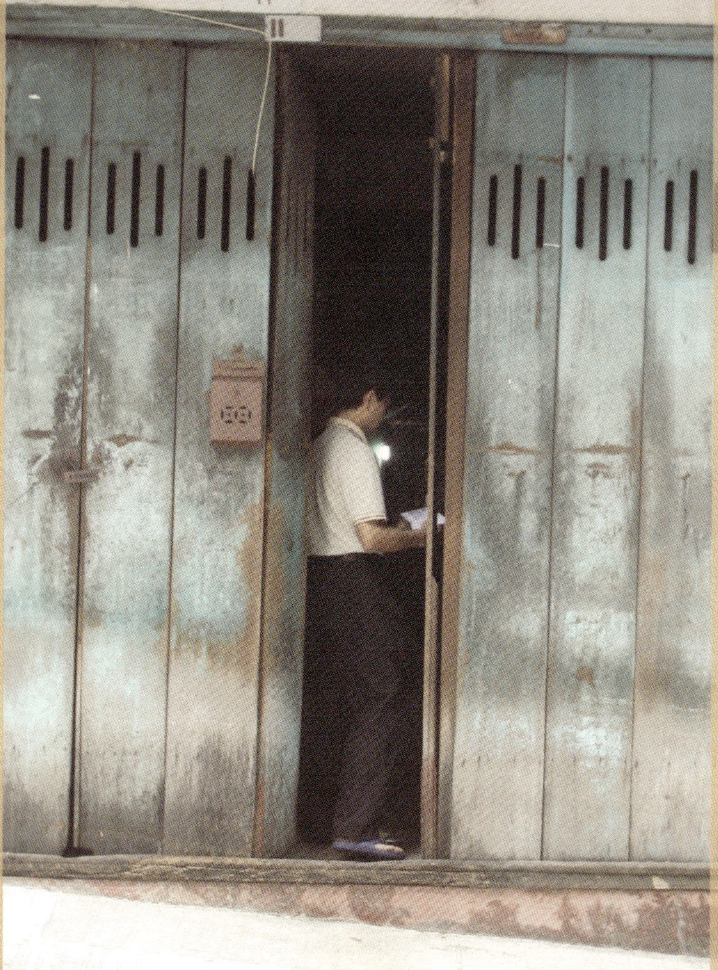

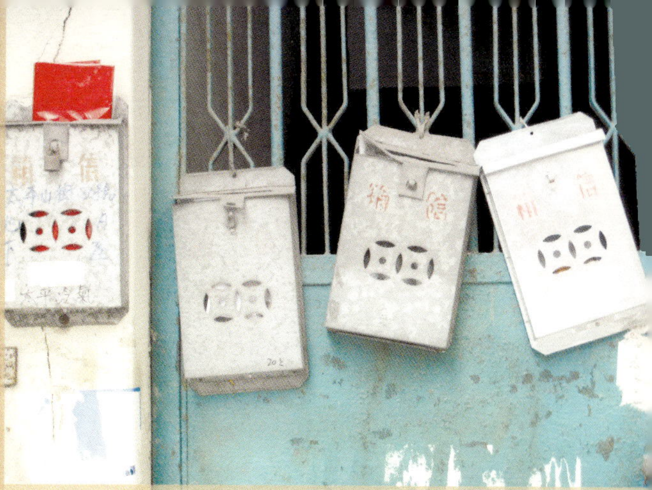

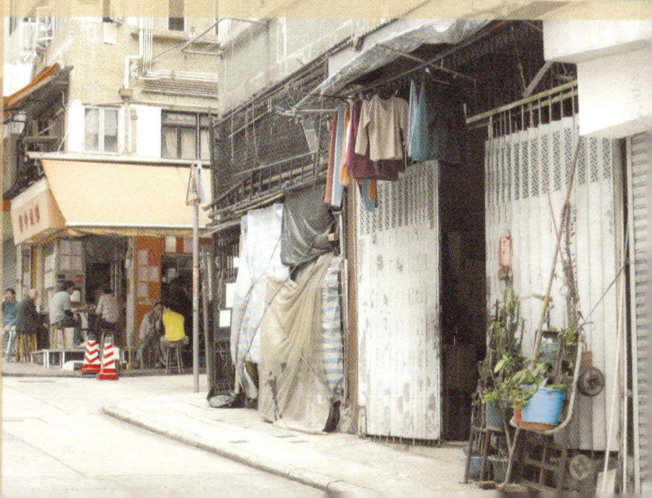

Mr. Yip

It was the bright blue gates, half-opened with a warm orange glow, that first led us to Mr. Yip's studio. I could tell someone was working away quietly inside — but on what and to what end? I found myself craning my neck to see until I finally gave up and just walked in.

Mr. Yip, a neatly-dressed man, looked up from behind his wooden desk; a friendly but curious smile crossing his face. Turns out, he's a silversmith, one of the last of his generation in Hong Kong. His speciality is making trophies.

"Which company in Hong Kong do you think needs the most trophies?" he asks.
"The Hong Kong Jockey Club?" I guess.
"*Lek lui, lek lui*," Mr. Yip laughs, repeating the Cantonese words for "smart girl."

Mr. Yip started working when he was 11; he was in his late 70s by the time we met on a cool December day in 2010. His employer, a century-old company in Central, Hong Kong's business district, sends him work whenever it's available. These days, that consists mostly of repairing silverware (he was ever so carefully mending a candle holder on this particular afternoon).

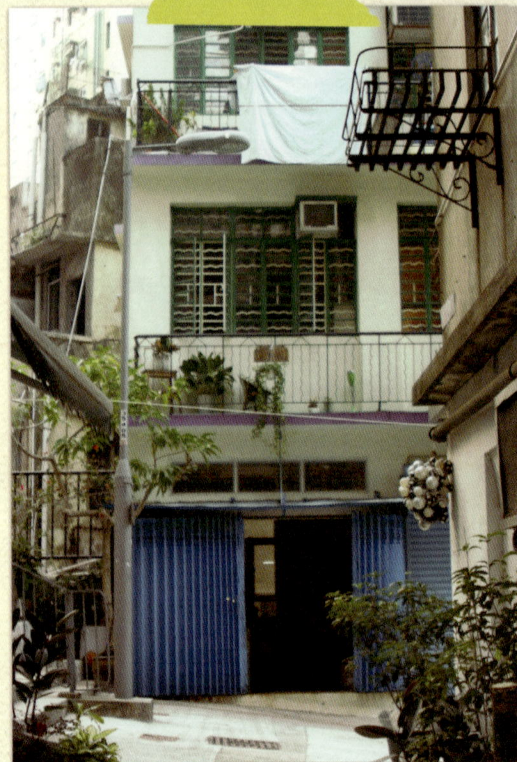

But there's not much demand for the craft of trophy-making any more, Mr. Yip continues, the radio playing softly in the background.

“Well, no,” he corrects himself. "It's not that there isn't demand. It's that we can't compete. Other companies use machines; we do it all by hand. We can't produce the same quantity or do it as cheaply. There's just me and a few others still left doing this. In the old days, there used to be many people just like me,” he says.

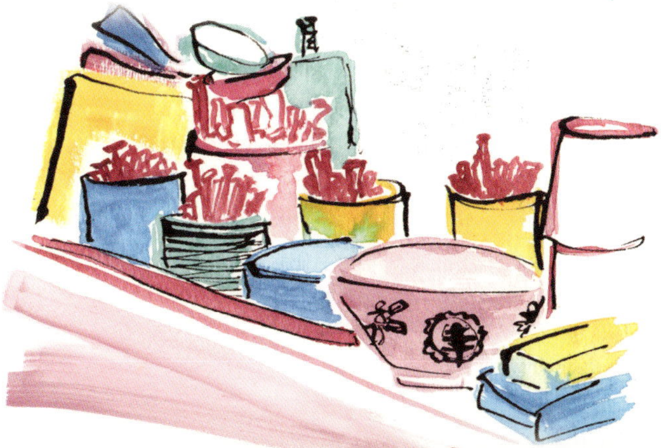

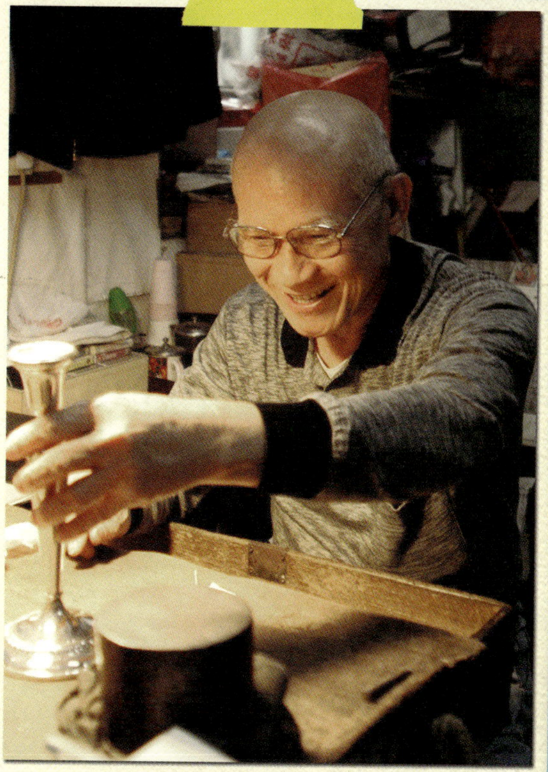

Detour off Hollywood Road

There were seniors manning stalls crammed to the hilt with Mao memorabilia, black-and-white photos of colonial Hong Kong and pretty Chinese door knobs. All made for tourists, of course, but I swooned nonetheless. Funny how you can live most of your life in a city, then discover as a returning tourist just how much you missed. I didn't even know where the Cat Street Bazaar was until I was 28, the year I married and brought Nick and a few friends to Hong Kong for our second wedding banquet.

My brother played tour guide that day, following directions in a tourism brochure that took us through the old herbalist streets of Sheung Wan, then up Possession Street to Hollywood Road. We detoured down to Cat Street (also known as Upper Lascar Row) and found a car-less lane with stalls running just a couple of blocks. Nick and I negotiated with an old granny for a print of old Hong Kong in all its rickshaw-laden glory. Then it was back up the stairs to Hollywood Road. Across the street was Man Mo Temple, one of Hong Kong's oldest and best-known temples, photo-op ready with heady smoke and spiralling incense.

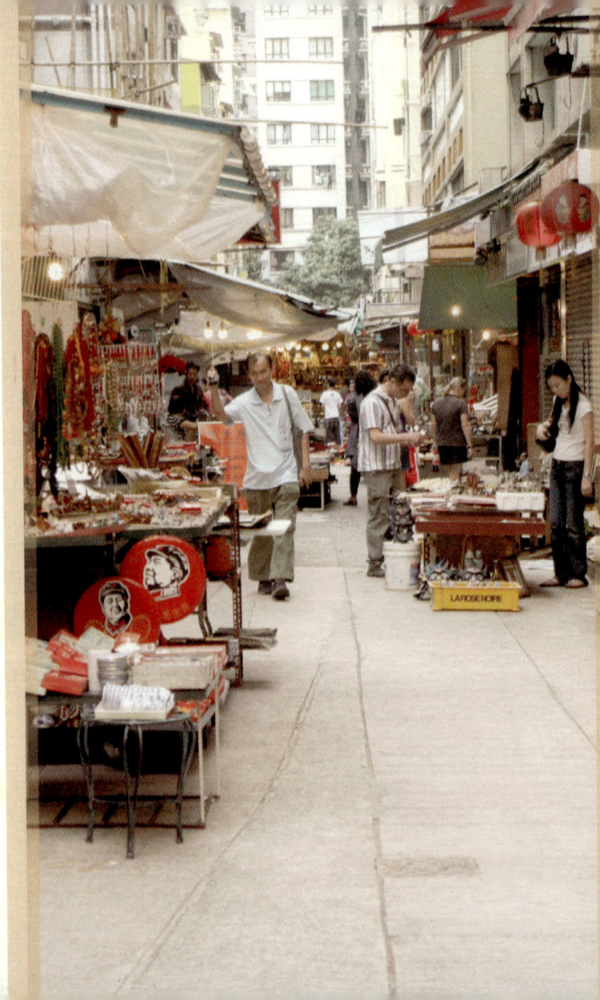

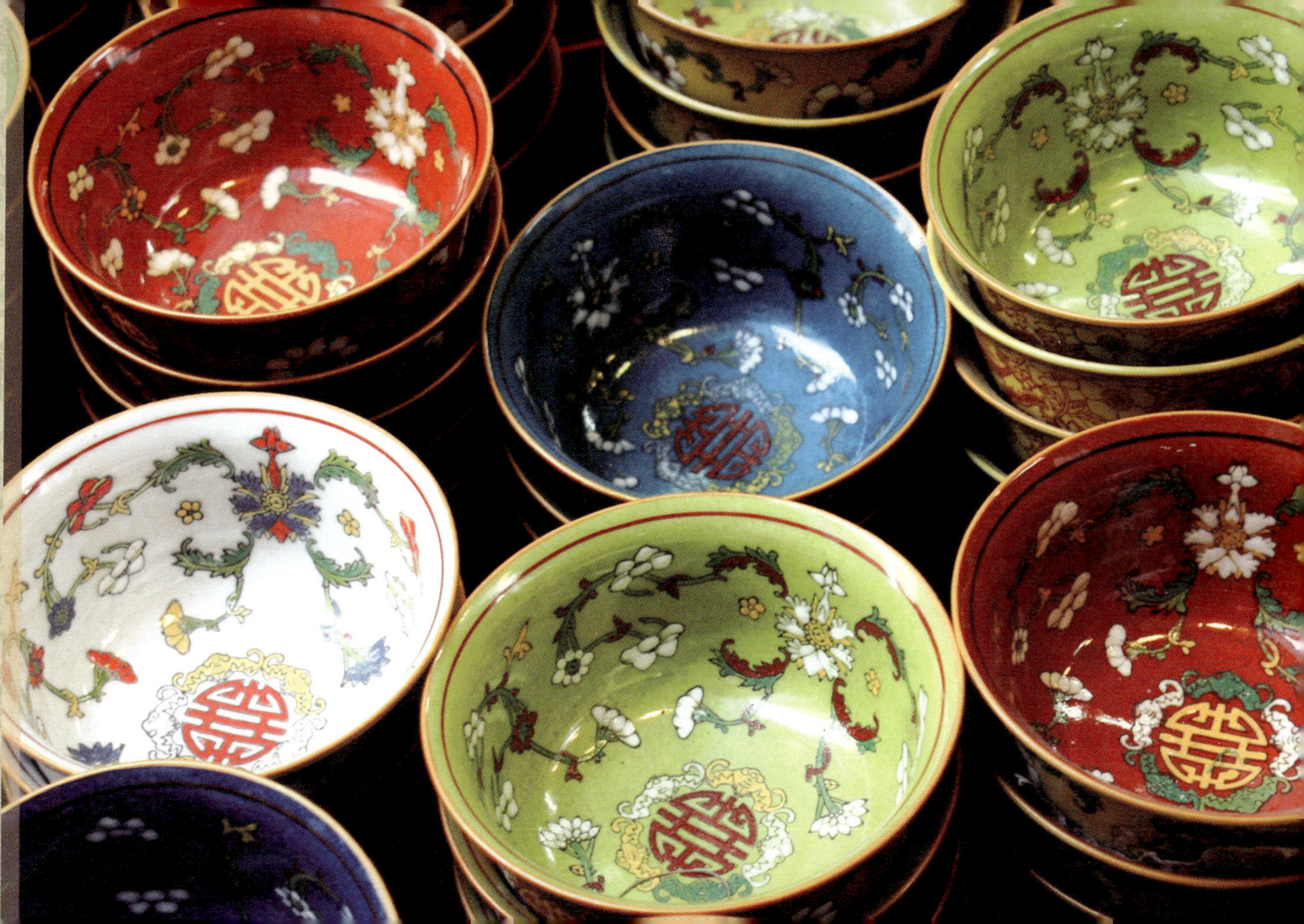

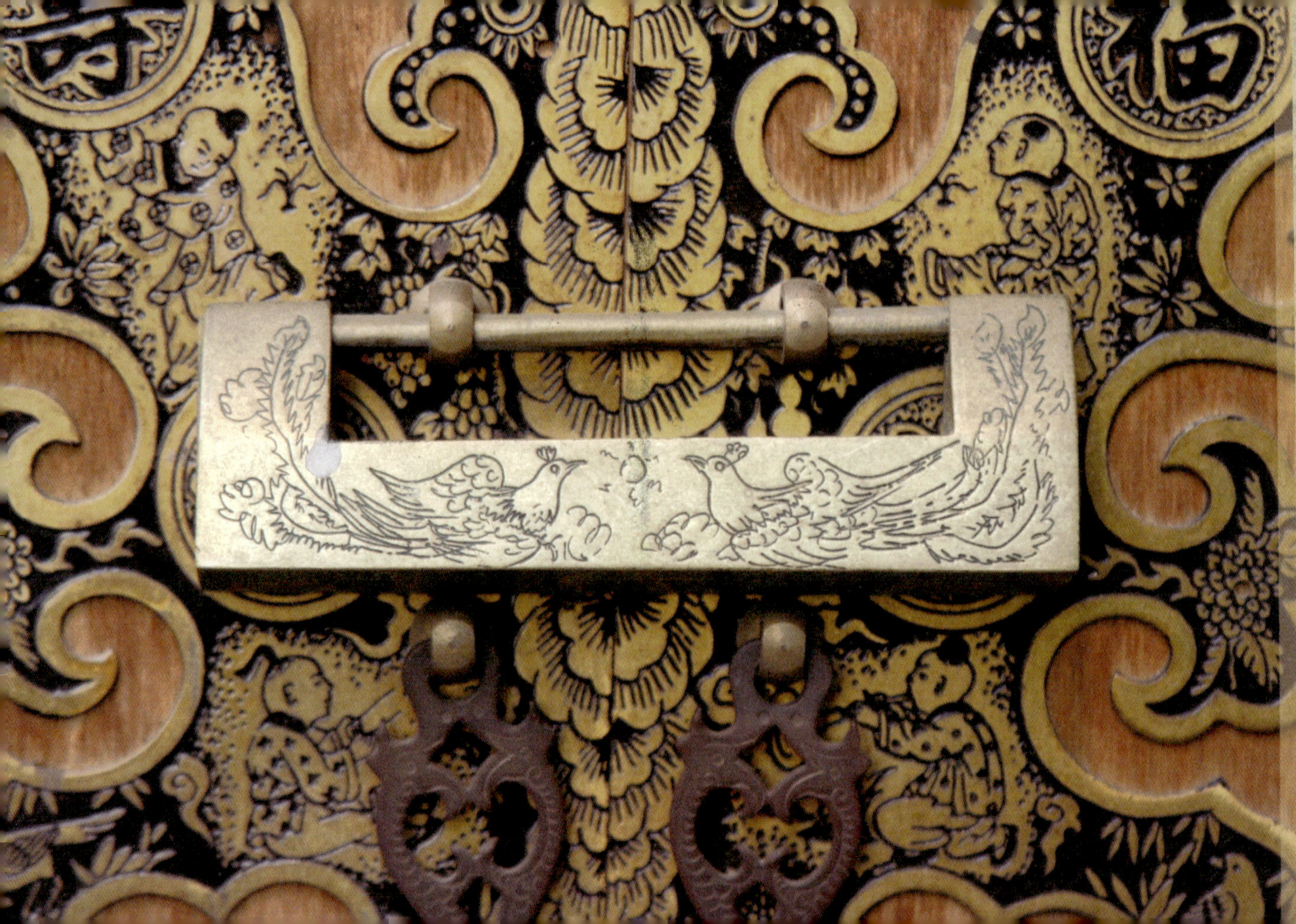

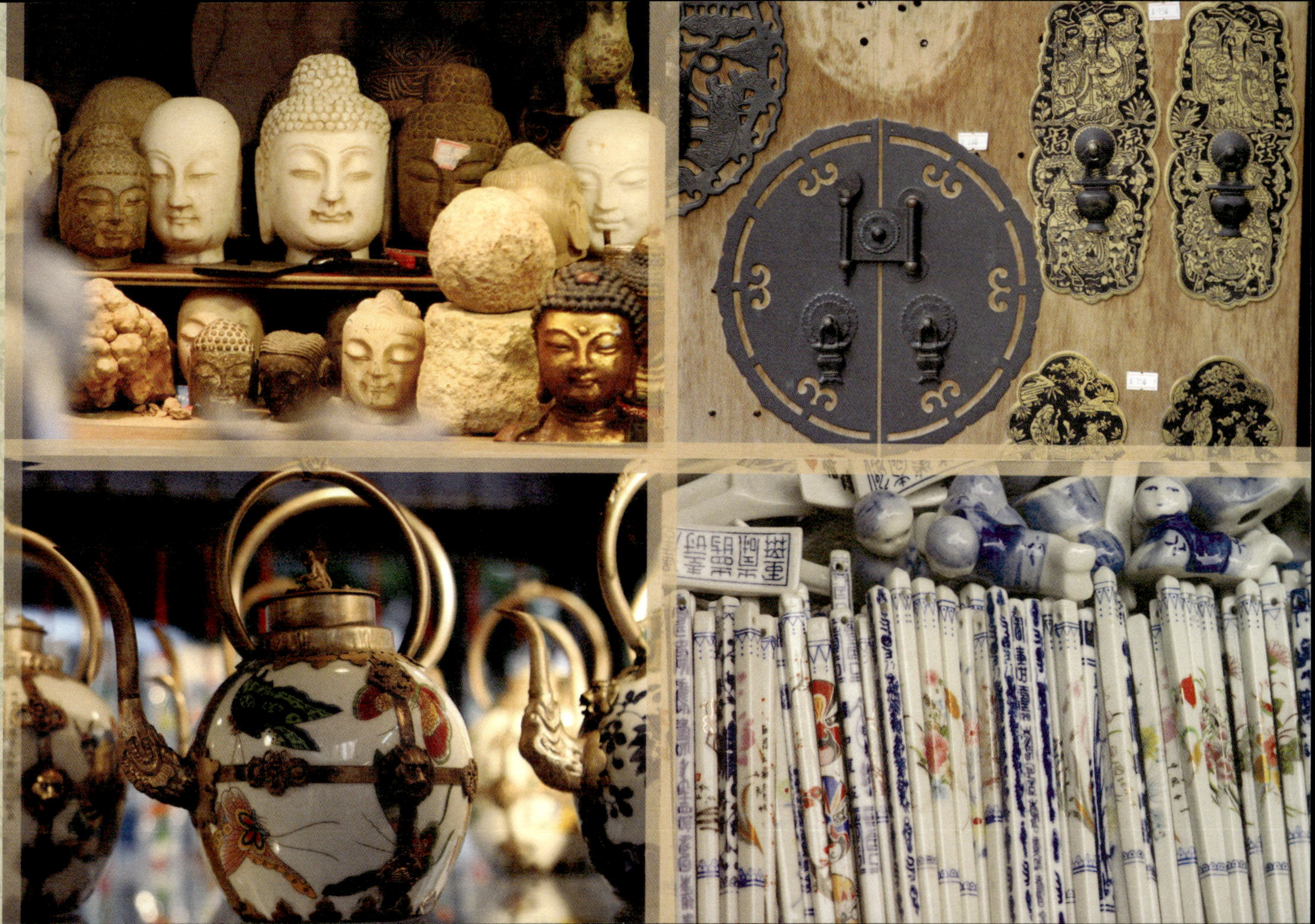
福禄
壽星

A Stroll Down Noho

The youthful, arty set have staked their claim on this tiny corner and named it Noho (North of Hollywood Road). The shift in energy is unmistakable, too, as we move from peaceful Sheung Wan to buzzy Central. Noho straddles the in-between.

It is essentially one street — Gough Street — though the boutiques spill over to Aberdeen Street too, where we once found ourselves stranded in a torrential rainstorm. As we waited for the storm to pass, we hopped from shop awning to shop awning, discovered vintage fashion at Bang! Bang! '70s and peered through the window of Moustache, whose elaborate displays were known to confuse some locals who routinely mistook it for an antique shop rather than a menswear boutique.

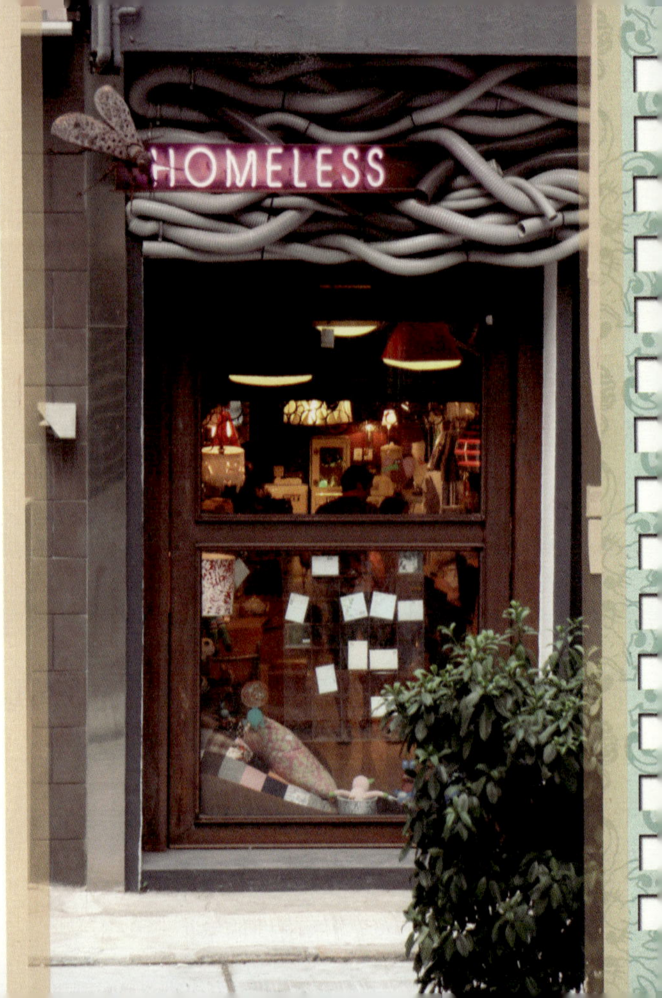

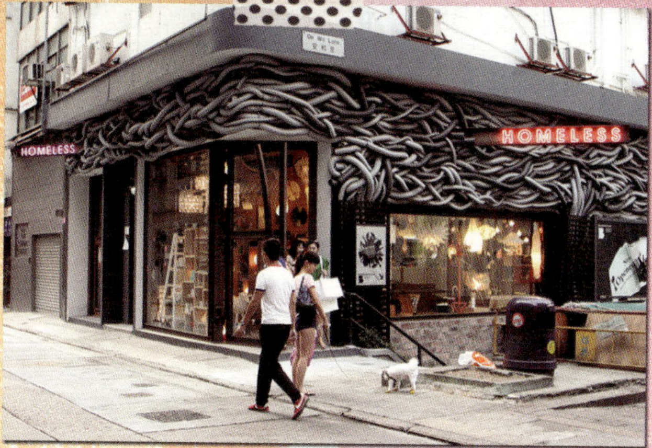
HOMELESS
HOMELESS

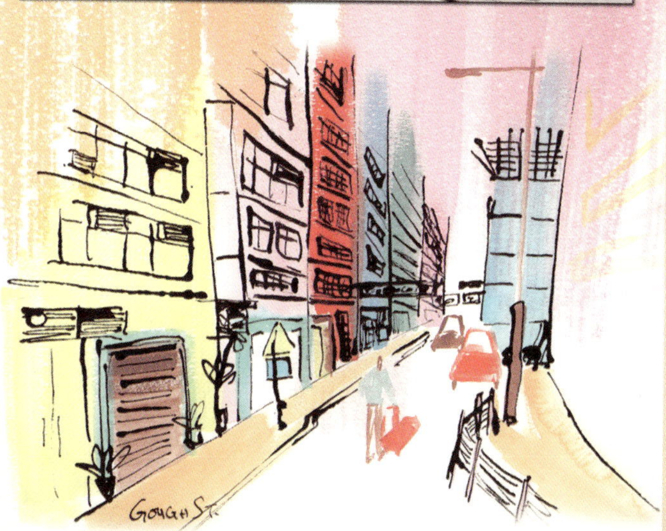
GOUGH ST.

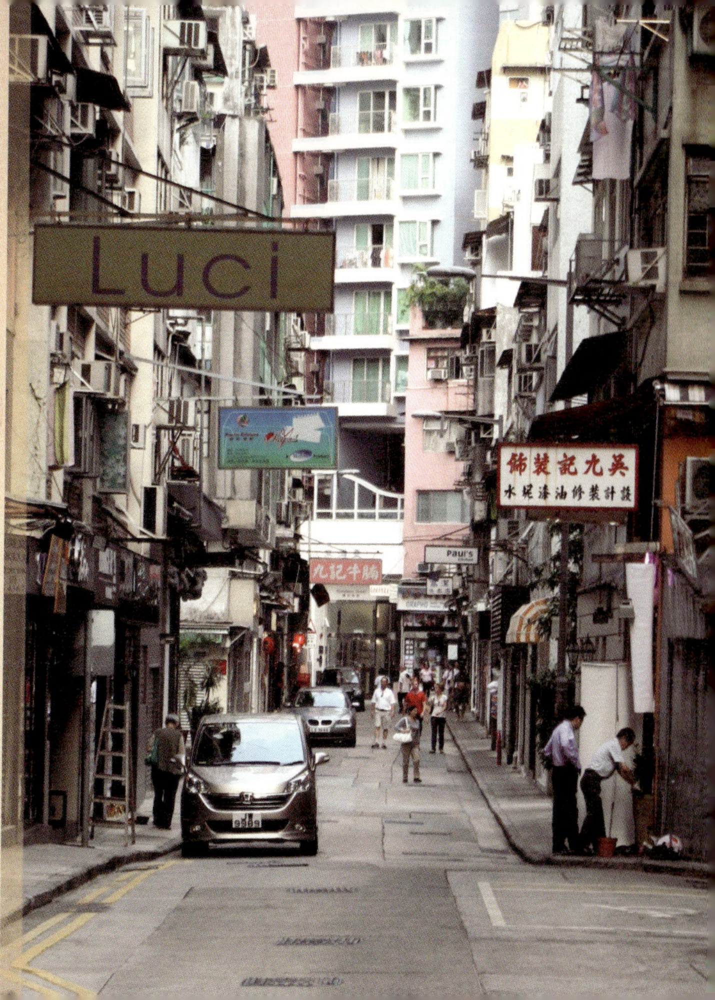
Luci
吳九記裝飾
設計裝修油漆泥水
Paul's

A Tailored Fit

On the bamboo rods hung beautifully tailored clothing wistful enough for a Wong Kar-Wai film. And though there was no mistaking the very Chinese-ness of the shop — a bust of Dr. Sun Yat-Sen graced the shop window and Chinese art adorned the painted brick walls — there was something almost revolutionary about the way the clothes articulated what it meant to dress *of the place.* Sometimes it takes an outsider's eye to catch what's really special about your city.

That "outsider," or outsiders rather, were Ellis Kreuger and Alex Daye, New Yorkers who created Moustache, a home-grown clothing line that quickly became known as one of the city's best. "We wanted to represent Hong Kong. We didn't want to be foreigners doing something foreign in Hong Kong," explains Ellis.

When the couple landed in Hong Kong in 2006, they were immediately drawn to the long-forgotten tailor shops this city was once famous for. They loved the personal service and surprisingly high level of craftsmanship on par with London's Savile Row and Milan's ateliers. But the boxy cuts and starchy fabrics? That, they could do without.

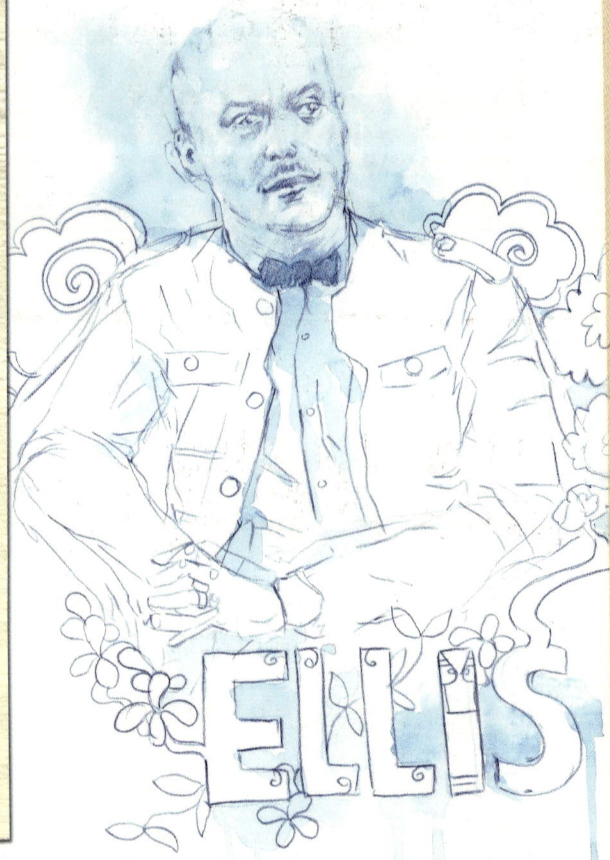

So why not marry a craft that was in danger of extinction with their keen eye for style? Despite a global economic meltdown in late 2008, the couple launched Moustache, a ready-to-wear and bespoke menswear line made of Indian cottons and Chinese silk. It didn't take long for Hong Kong's sartorial set to respond in kind, financial tsunami be damned.

"The first prototypes we made were the dream things that we wanted to own," says Ellis. "We also wanted to have what we did be about Hong Kong. We love Wong Kar-Wai in *In the Mood for Love* and *2046* so our house cut is very early 1960s tailoring, and we really wanted to tell that story and wake people up to this amazing level of craftsmanship here in Hong Kong, and in Kowloon, too. Not the 24-hour suits made across the border, but the really time-honoured Hong Kong tailoring."

Although there are hundreds of tailors in the city, Ellis estimates there are only about 10 master craftsmen left. Partnering with them was not just about preserving a craft, but also sharing knowledge and skill. "It's very much a mutual thing with the people who make our clothing because you learn from them too," he says. "It's a swapping of skills."

It was easy to fall in love with Moustache's brand of romanticism: the way they noticed every tiny detail of the

Alex and Ellis created this guide book to point the way to their favourite Hong Kong spots. We love it!

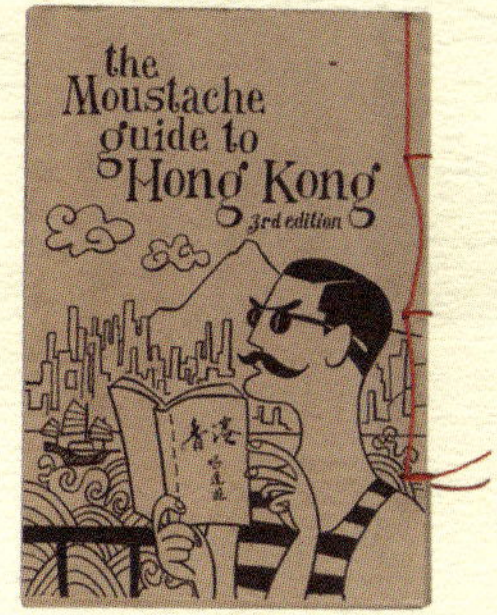

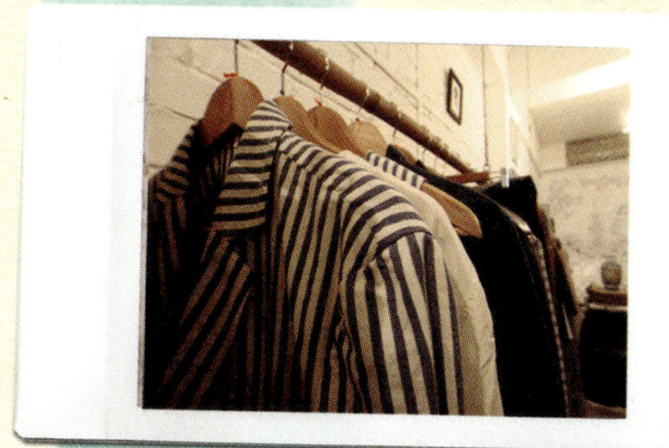

They redecorated the shop annually.

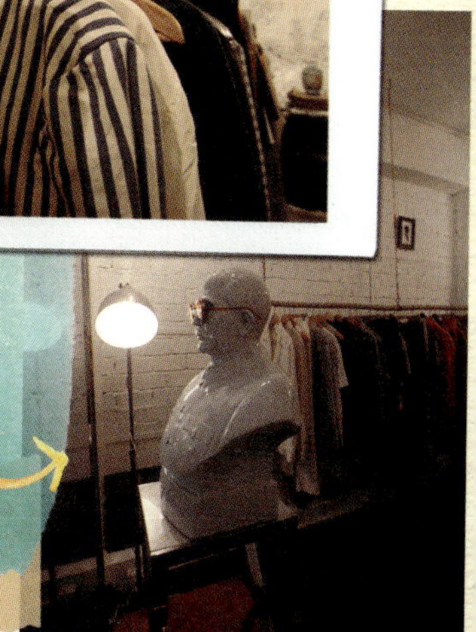

landscape, from the particular turquoise of the delivery trucks to the tiny beach villages which inspired their collections. Their clothes hinted at British dandyism while paying homage to retro Hong Kong style.

Ellis describes Moustache as "happy circumstance." After seven years as a designer at New York brand Tocca, he came to Hong Kong to work for a fashion label. But the corporate environment and 16-hour days were a "nightmare." Rather than return to New York, they decided to stay put and ride out the rest of the year given the heavy contractual agreement Ellis had signed. "And in that year, although the job and work kind of sucked, we fell in love with the city," he says.

When asked what they love most about Hong Kong, Ellis is quick to point out "it's not a complete love affair."

"It's more of a roller-coaster ride of highs and lows, but there's nothing mediocre about it," he laughs. "Sometimes the nature thing gets me. It's like driving around the island and it's just mountains and water. The markets, I'm always struck by how great the food is here."

"I think it's also the possibilities," adds Alex. "Particularly at this moment there seems to be a real 'let's do something' mentality. . . People try things, sometimes it's great, sometimes it's not so great. It's very creative."

Hong Kong has always been defined by the adventurers who come here, drawn by the chance to create something new and wholly their own. That also means this city is, by nature, transient. After eight years, the couple were ready for their next adventure. Their next stop: Sydney. While tastemakers mourned the closing of Moustache in December 2014, there was little doubt they left this city a little more certain of just what it meant to swagger with Hong Kong style.

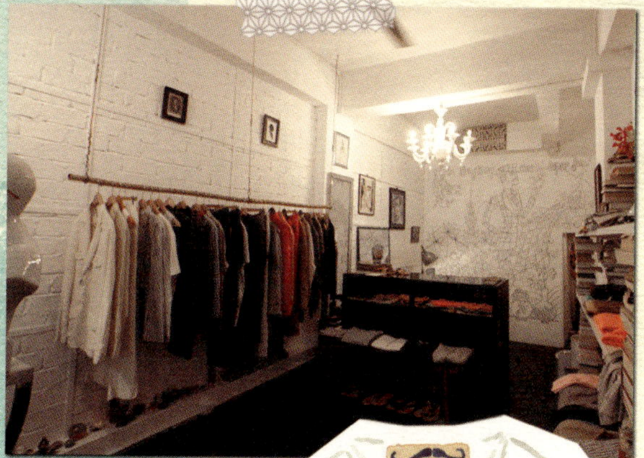

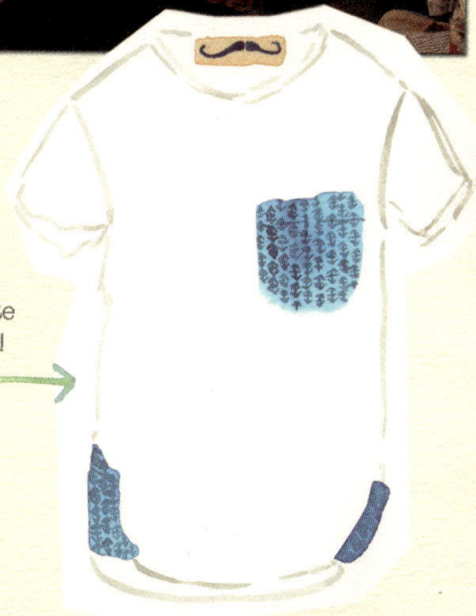

Nick's favourite
Moustache tee!

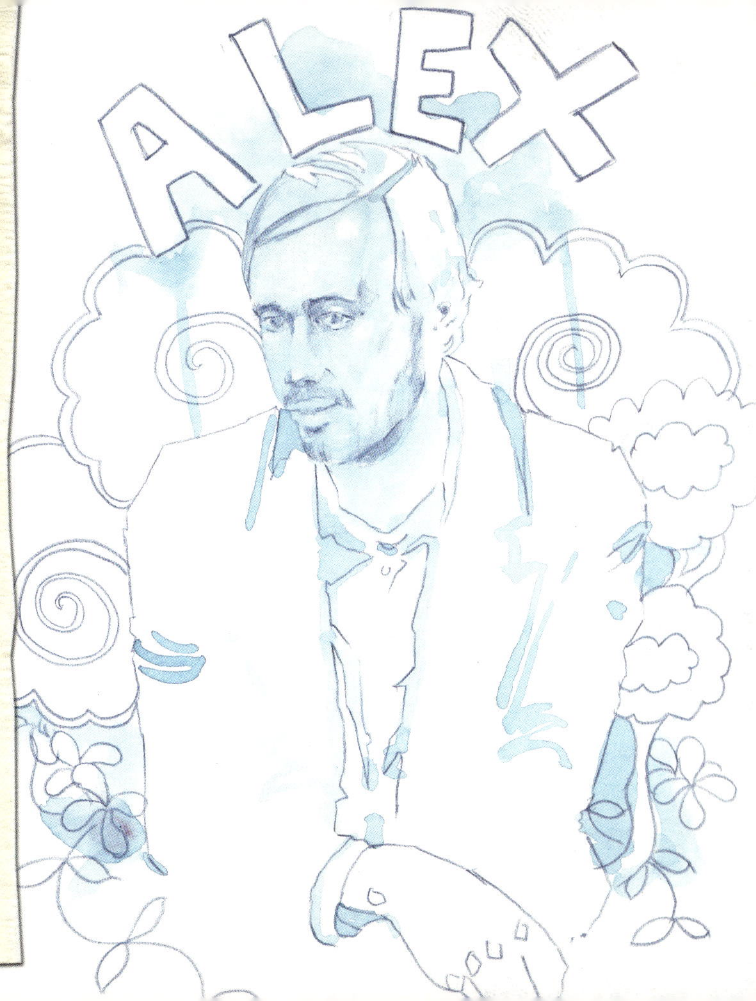

Go Modern

in

Central

Brassy, Brash Heart

I must admit, I tried not to love Central. I mean, if the point was to open a window into Hong Kong's soul, then surely this was not it. Soaring architecture, glass and concrete, power suits, marching office workers, *tai tais* and lots and lots of expats. Sure, there's something impressive about it — this is, after all, the financial centre of the city — but what about its *soul*?

Something, however, kept nagging at me. And that's when I realized, in my misguided attempt to document *authentic* — in a city with so many faces, what is that anyway? — I was denying myself the opportunity to just love what I love.

Ironically, the very place I wanted to shun was probably the place I'd spent the most time in my adolescence. Returning to Hong Kong from Canada at age seven with only a basic knowledge of Cantonese meant there was no way I could attend a local school; instead, I was enrolled in an international school. Most of my friends were expat kids and Central was, and remains, expat headquarters with organic juice bars, yoga studios and, of course, the boozy corner of Lan Kwai Fong, the best place to make a few poor decisions. No, perhaps not the most "local" part of town, but one that's part and parcel of the fabric of this former British colony.

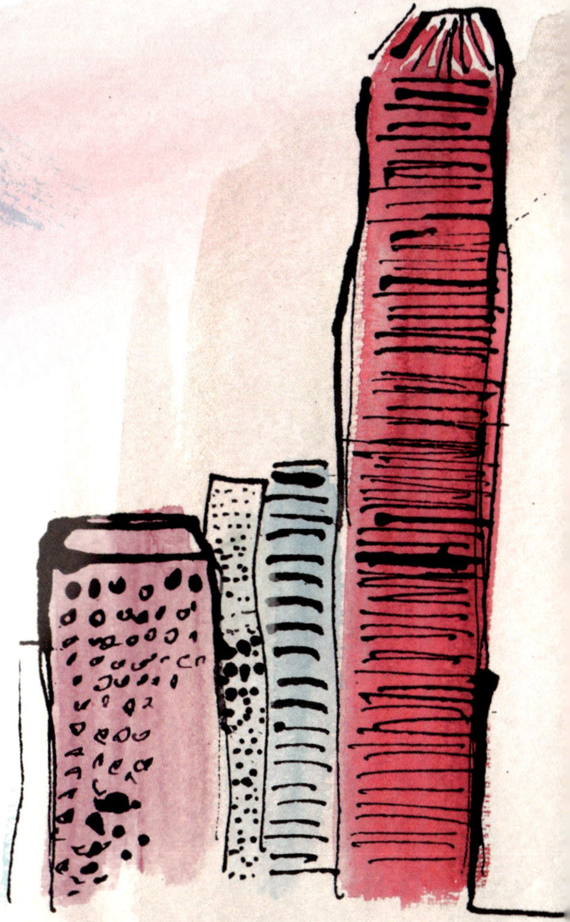

These days, I love Central mostly for the lazy Sundays I spend here with my family, eating dim sum then meandering the strangely quiet streets, poking around in stores with almost nobody in them. For the art galleries along Hollywood Road and even the admittedly swish eateries in Soho. For Lan Kwai Fong too, even though I've outgrown the bar-hopping madness, it's still a trip to come by from time to time. For "the Lanes" as they're known, especially the little stall at the end where I always pick up a few cheap and cheerful cardies. Shanghai Tang, Pedder Building, Graham Street, Ladder Street. Yep, love, love and love. I.M. Pei's Bank of China building with its angles and triangles and the iconic ifc clawing into the sky — where would the city be without these architectural icons? So this is Central. Unabashed, unapologetic Central. I hope you love it, too.

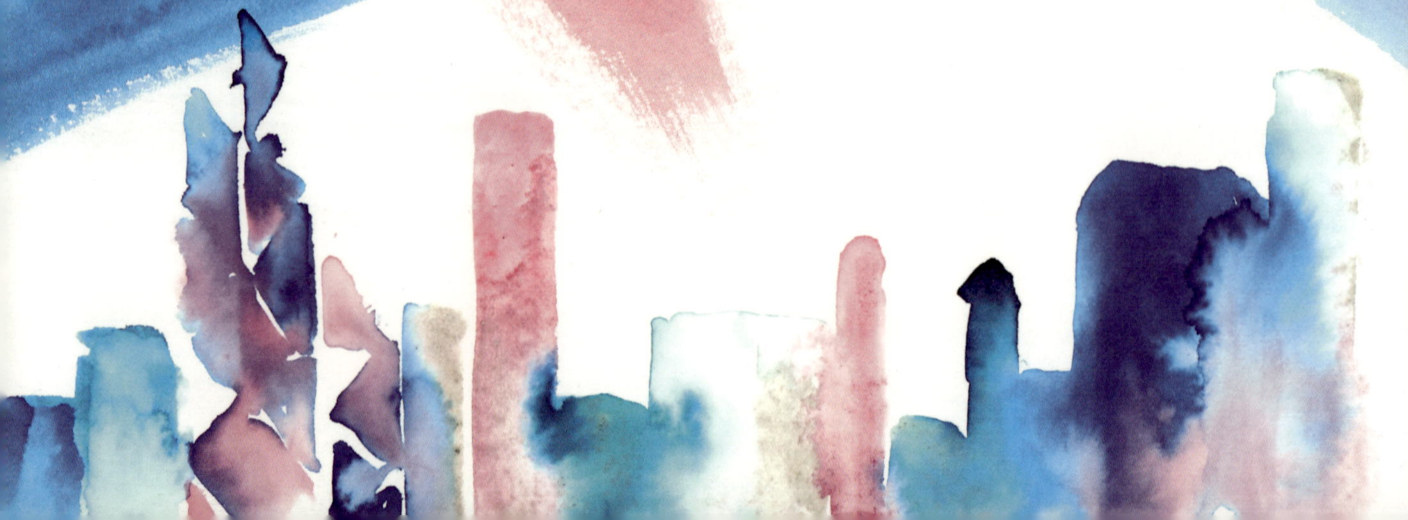

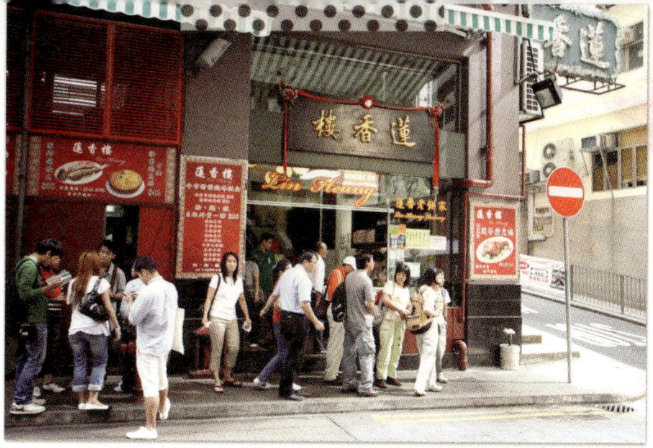

Above: Lin Heung, an old teahouse popular with locals, but not for the faint of heart. Expect to share tables and do lots of elbowing to get to the dim sum carts.

Right: The iconic Star Ferry with Hong Kong's famous skyline behind.

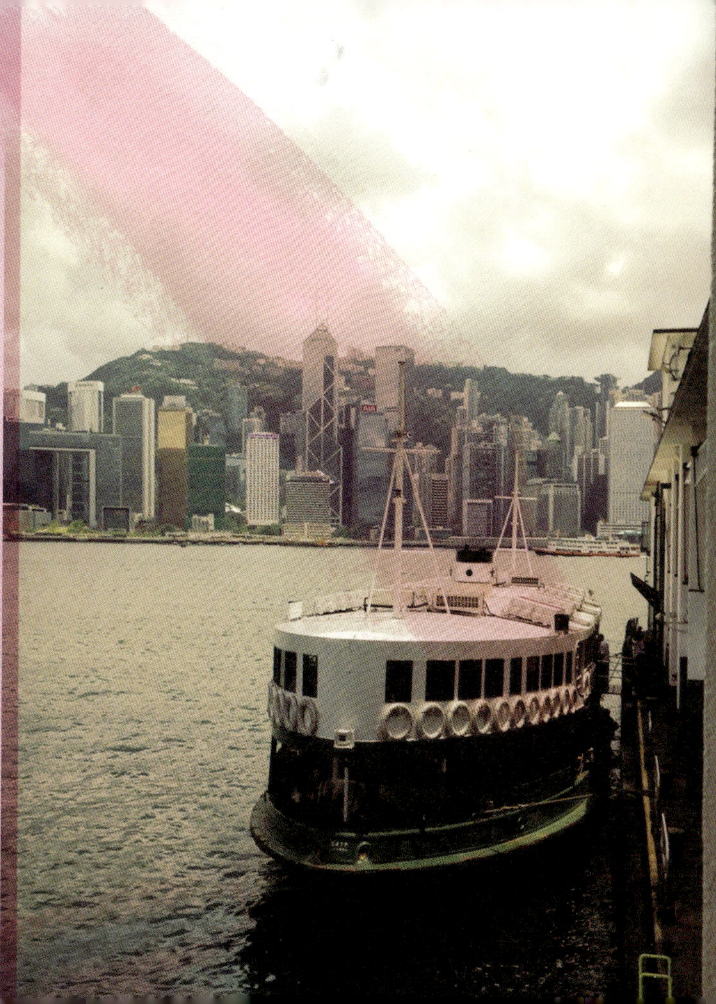

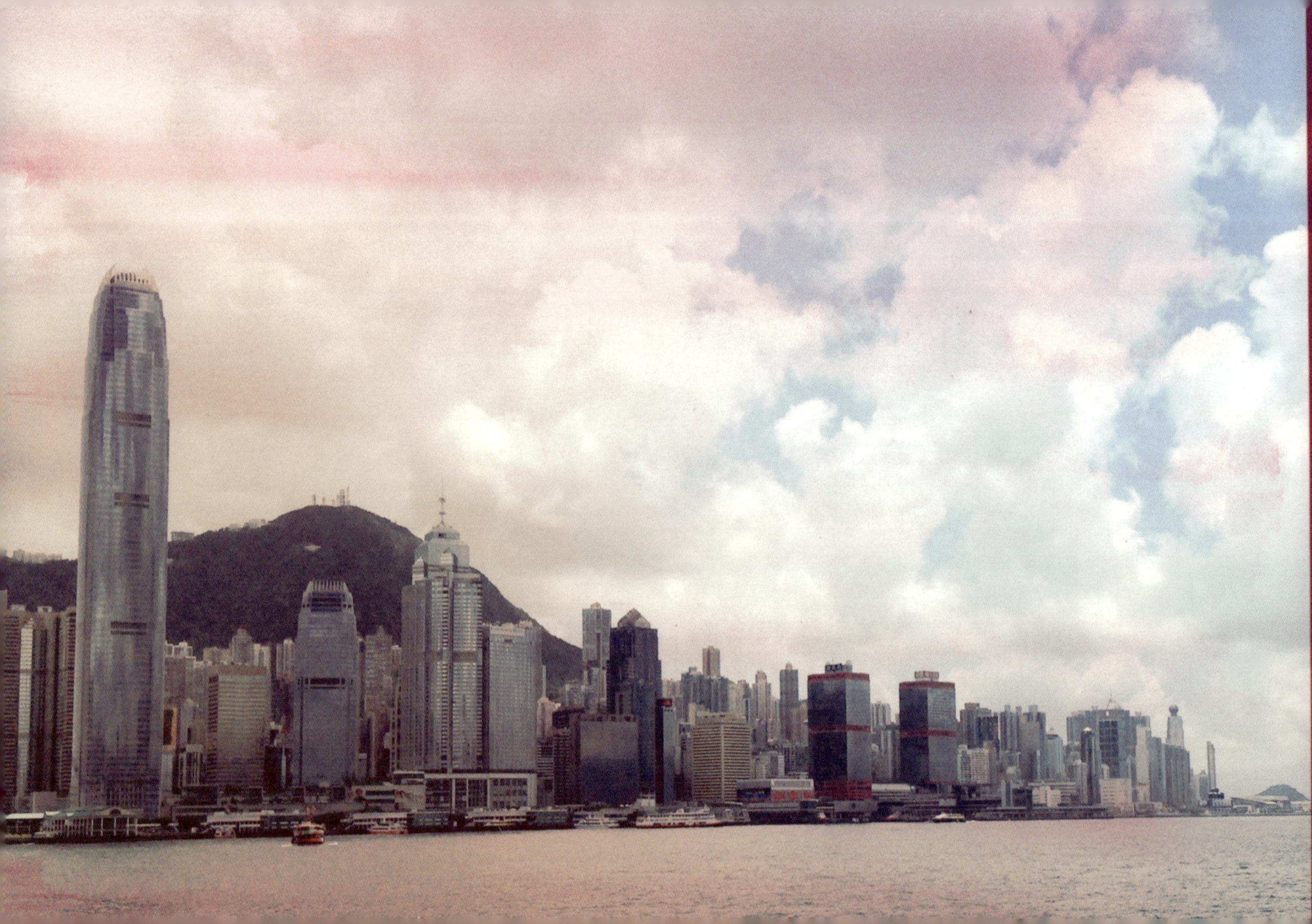

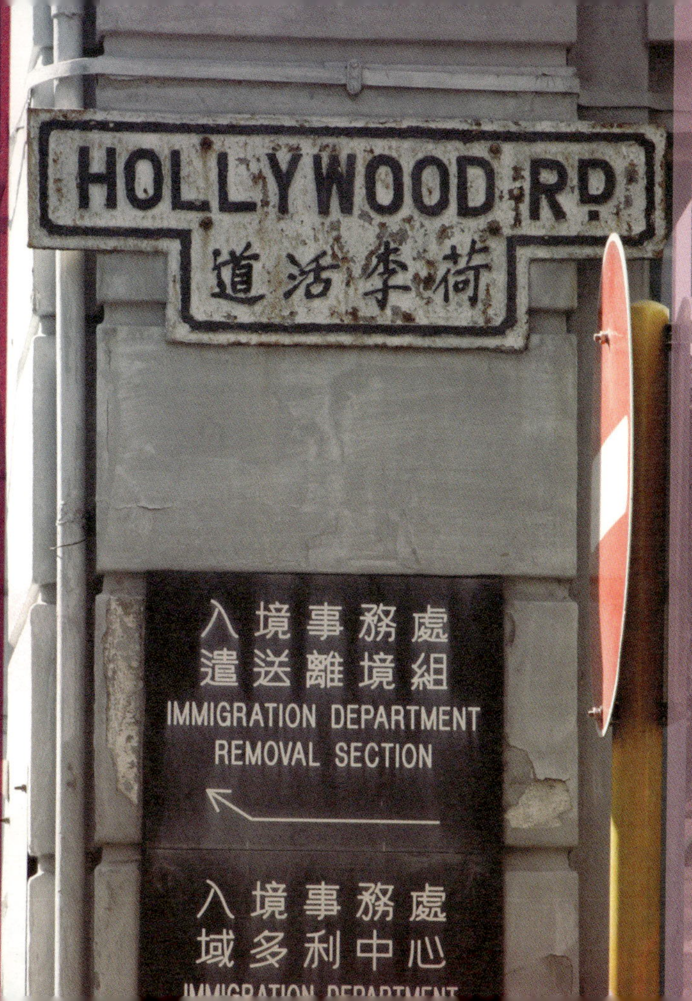
HOLLYWOOD RD
荷李活道
入境事務處
遣送離境組
IMMIGRATION DEPARTMENT
REMOVAL SECTION
入境事務處
域多利中心

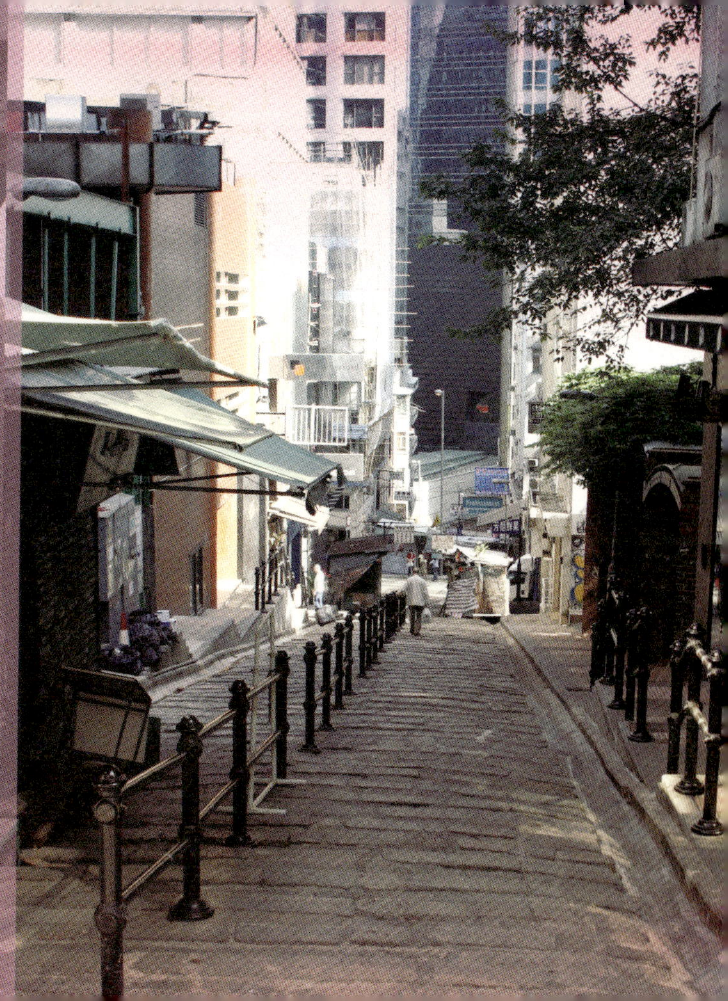

The Scent of my Youth

What's that intoxicating scent as you walk through the doors? Why, it's ginger flower of course, the very same spicy sweet fragrance that made me fall in love with Shanghai Tang in the first place. One whiff and I'm brought back to the wooden floors, dark interiors and stained-glass windows of its stately store. I was 14 and couldn't afford anything in there, so I inhaled this olfactory bliss instead.

It was the mid-1990s when Shanghai Tang arrived on the scene, a time when Hong Kongers were anticipating the return of the British colony to China in 1997. Patriotism and fear were both running high. Shanghai Tang took the former by its collar and ran with it in brilliant, technicoloured fashion. They made wearing *cheongsams* cool. They made mandarin collars cool. They took the fresh, springtime seduction of the white ginger lily and turned it into something both exotic and celebratory. Oriental chic in a bottle.

Two decades later and I'm still in love with Shanghai Tang, and Shanghai Tang's still in love with China. I love the thoughtfulness behind their designs, each piece taking its cue from the history and landscape of the country (see that wavy pattern on that silk dress? It's inspired by rice fields in China). They were the first fashion and lifestyle company, in my memory at least, to celebrate Chinese style in such a big

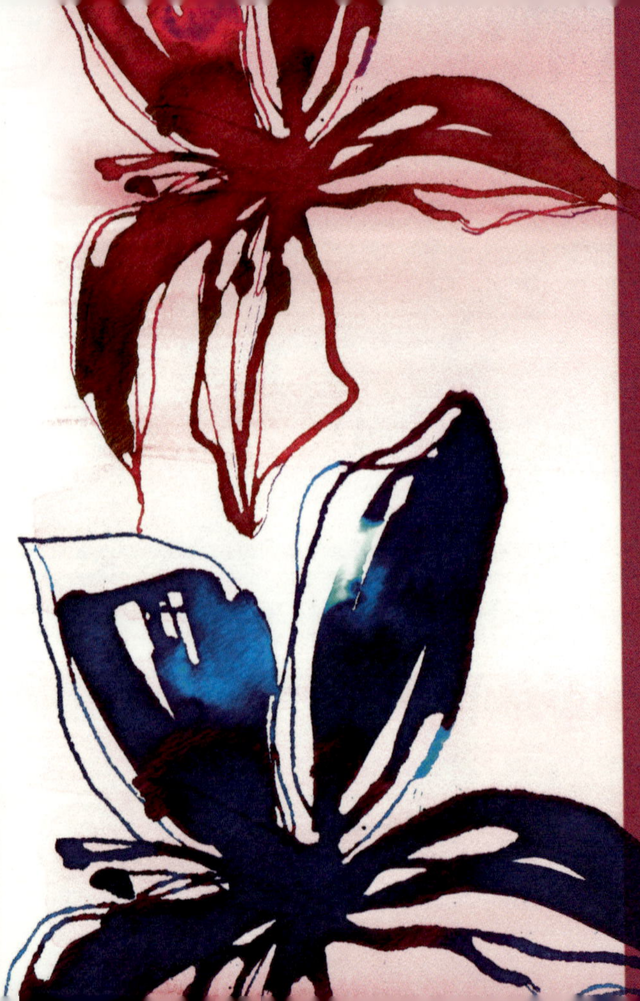

way. I miss the old-world feel of their first store in the stone-clad Pedder Building (the new one's too flash for my taste). But for showing the world how sophisticated and fun Chinese design can be, I think I will always love Shanghai Tang.

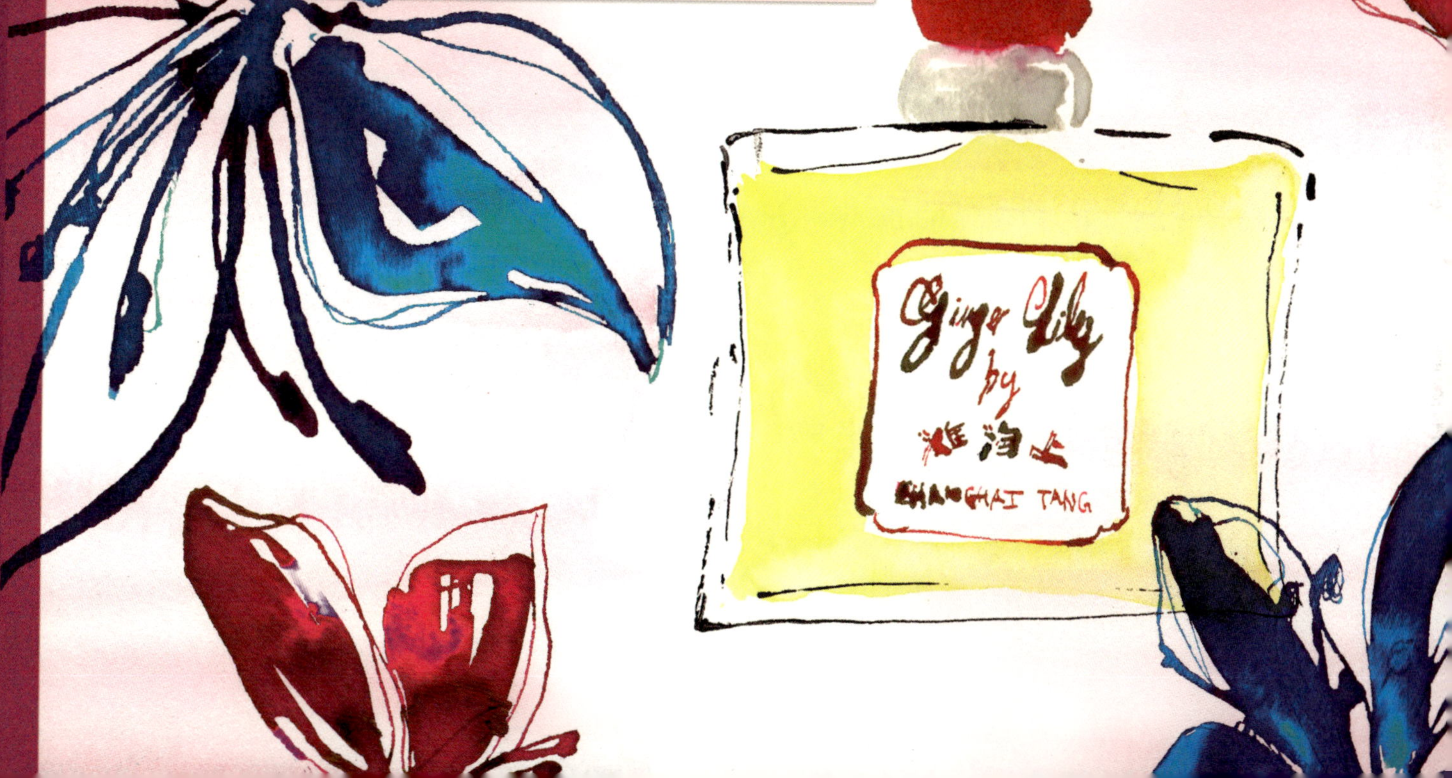

Remember When. . .

We were walking down Graham Street Market after brunch and discovered a stall selling doll-sized, wooden Chinese furniture? *"Only in Hong Kong!"* my girlfriend exclaimed at the strange but wonderful discovery.

My American colleague asked if I grew up here. I said yes. "Must've been one helluva playground," he replied.

7-Eleven microwaveable dim sum was the *best thing ever*? Especially when hung over.

We were hanging out after school, on a tiny patch of grass next to the mall. We laid down and looked up at the skyscrapers surrounding us and I knew even then *how lucky* I was to live here.

A friend of mine once said that the ***bauhinia****, a pink tropical flower native to the city, was chosen as the flower of Hong Kong because it can thrive in even the most arduous circumstances. While I have never been able to verify this myth, the legend no doubt captures the essence of Hong Kong.*

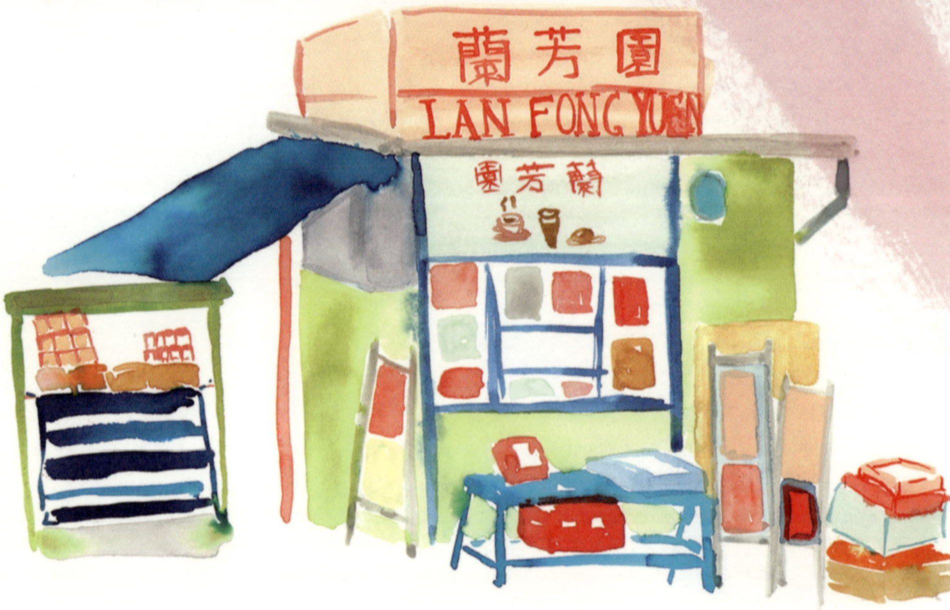

Lan Fong Yuen

Famished? Feet dragging? Need a caffeine fix? We know the feeling. Our weary bodies found this hole-in-the-wall quite by accident. We were tired, needed a break and so we sauntered in and perched our bottoms on round wooden stools. We ordered thick French toast dripping in melting icebergs of butter and caffeinated ourselves with sweet milk tea. The waiters erred on the side of surly. This is a classic Hong Kong *cha chaan teng*, sort of a diner-meets-teahouse. We found out later this place was famous.

The Longest Escalator

Once upon a time, these noodle-thin streets straddling the border of Sheung Wan and Central were nothing but a rundown grid home to grannies and grandpas who held onto traditions such as paper- and lantern-making and other crafts and trades. And though they occupied prime city land, nobody seemed to bother them much. But then came the escalator — and not just any escalator, but the longest one in the world. Built in 1994, the 800-metre-long conveyor connected the business district of Central to the upscale residential enclave of Mid Levels up above on the hillside. Along the way, it cut a swathe through these old streets and soon enough, pricey bars and chi-chi restaurants invaded, along with a yuppie crowd of locals and expats.

Today, the debate over gentrification has long passed (that it's called Soho at all — short for South of Hollywood Road — should give you a clue). Still, even today Soho can elicit wildly polarizing views from visitors and locals alike. Some say it could be anywhere in the world with its western-style eateries and English-speaking shops. Others love it for its quiet boutiques by day and boozy, convivial atmosphere by night. We've felt both ends of the spectrum depending on the day. We think it's still a side of Hong Kong that's worth a gander. How long you stay is up to you.

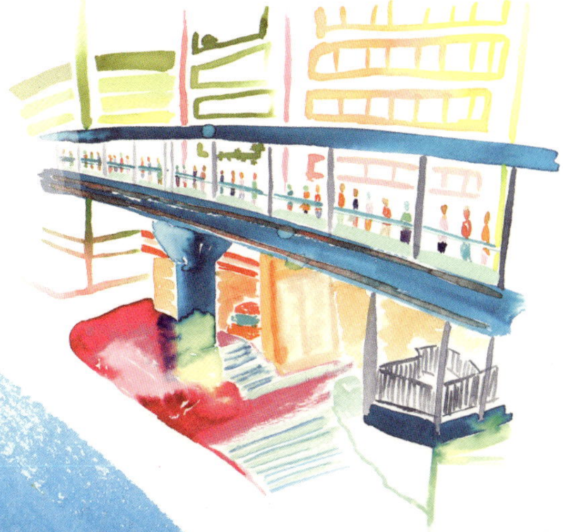

MADE IN HONG KONG

Walking into G.O.D. for the first time was like having someone walk into my head, extricate my love for this city, then reimagine it in the form of a shop. G.O.D. is often described as a lifestyle store selling home decor, books and clothing. But it's above all an ode to Hong Kong, capturing its past and present with humour and wit, and quite often taking me back to childhood memories I had nearly forgotten. Even the name is a phonetic play on the store's Cantonese name, *ju ho dee*, which means to live better. We tracked down founder Douglas Young to talk shop about G.O.D. and Hong Kong style.

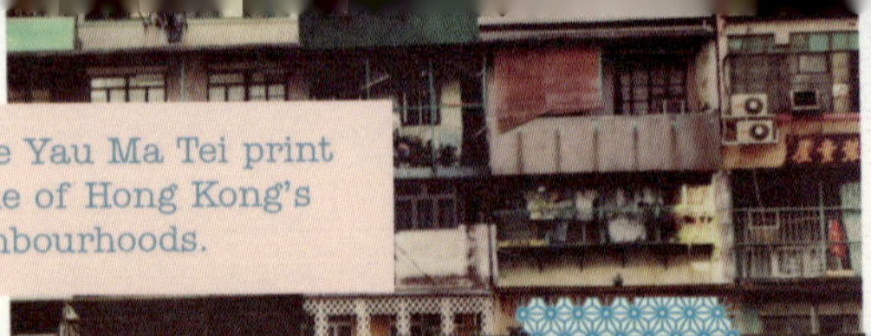

The signature Yau Ma Tei print celebrates one of Hong Kong's densest neighbourhoods.

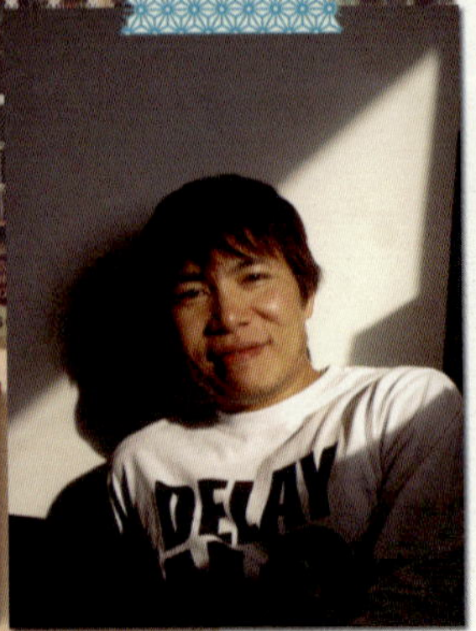

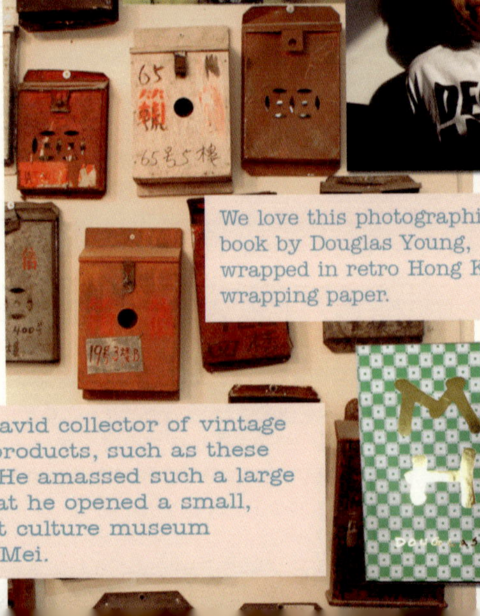

Young is an avid collector of vintage Hong Kong products, such as these letterboxes. He amassed such a large collection that he opened a small, quirky street culture museum in Shek Kip Mei.

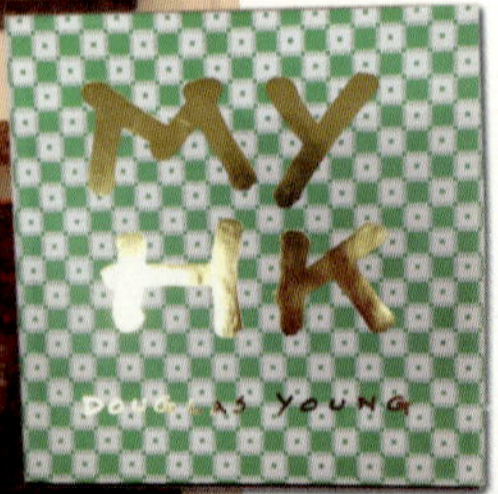

We love this photographic book by Douglas Young, wrapped in retro Hong Kong wrapping paper.

G.O.D. really captures the heart and soul of Hong Kong. Can you tell us about the special relationship you have with the city?
Hong Kong is both somewhere familiar (because I grew up here) and foreign (because I spent a number of years away from it). I can see things only tourists see, as well as things only locals can see.

How did the idea for G.O.D. come to you?
Hong Kong is crying out for a brand that is inspired by local culture. Indigenous culture is the essence behind all the world's greatest brands.

What do you want people to feel when they walk through the doors of G.O.D.?
That they are in a miniaturized version of Hong Kong.

What's the essence of Hong Kong style?
Hong Kong style is about the clash of things that are incongruent.

What inspires you?
Irony.

What makes you most proud of being a Hong Konger?
That we can still survive (just).

Hong Kong in a word. . .
Delaynomore!

Is Hong Kong a city you've always felt great affection for, or was it something you developed later in life?
No, two minutes ago I hated it, now I love it, but I cannot guarantee what I will feel 10 minutes later.

The perfect way to spend a Sunday?
I like to go to work on a Sunday, the telephones are very quiet.

Favourite restaurant?
Seafood on sampans at the typhoon shelter (but it doesn't exist any more).

How do you see the city evolving?
Hong Kong will evolve to be a city where creativity will play an important role.

What's the allure of Hong Kong? Why does it capture so many people's imagination?
Dollars.

Star Ferry and the Space Between

What makes the Star Ferry so compelling? Could it be its storied history, its rickety benches, or the journey itself, traversing the famous 'Fragrant Harbour' for which this city is named? Or maybe it's just that for a brief moment, you're suspended between states of mind. On one side is bustling Central, all business-like and towering into the sky, its gleaming spires dripping with efficiency and money. On the other is maddening Tsim Sha Tsui, peopled on every corner, crowded, chaotic and ready for a good time. But here, in the space between, you can breathe, contemplate, really see the beauty that is all around you. Whether chugging towards Hong Kong or Kowloon, the Star Ferry never fails to put everything in perspective. From here, at this fleeting point on this fabled harbour, I am routinely struck by the beauty of the skyline and lulled by the peacefulness of the water. The Star Ferry has been loved for generations. Steadfast and reliable, it's been in service since 1880. In a city as transitory as Hong Kong, few things are imbued with as much sentimentality as this.

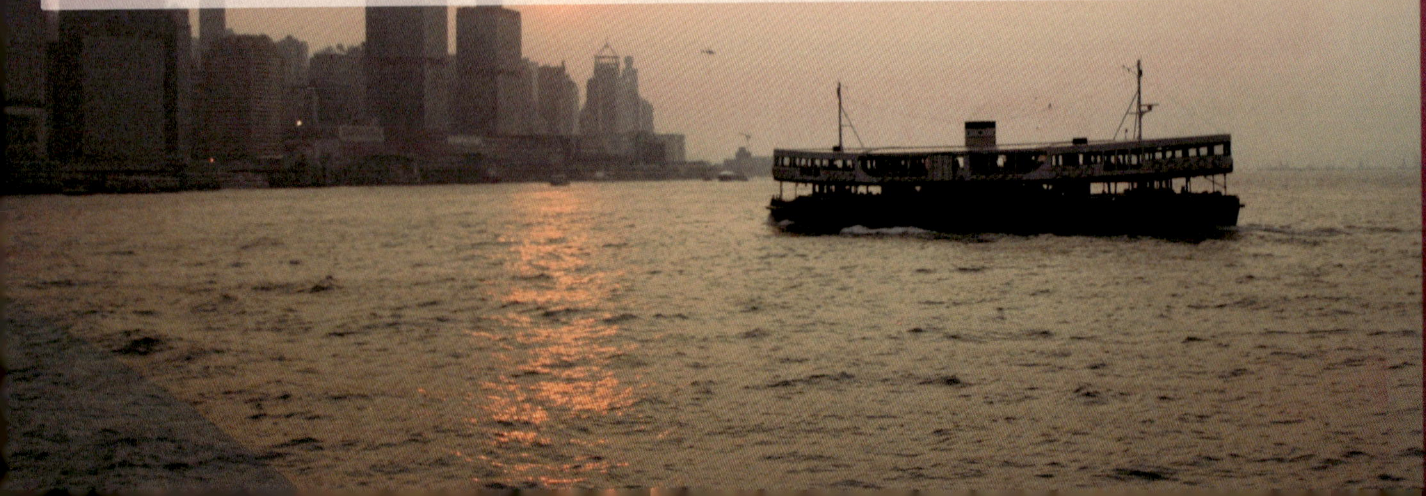

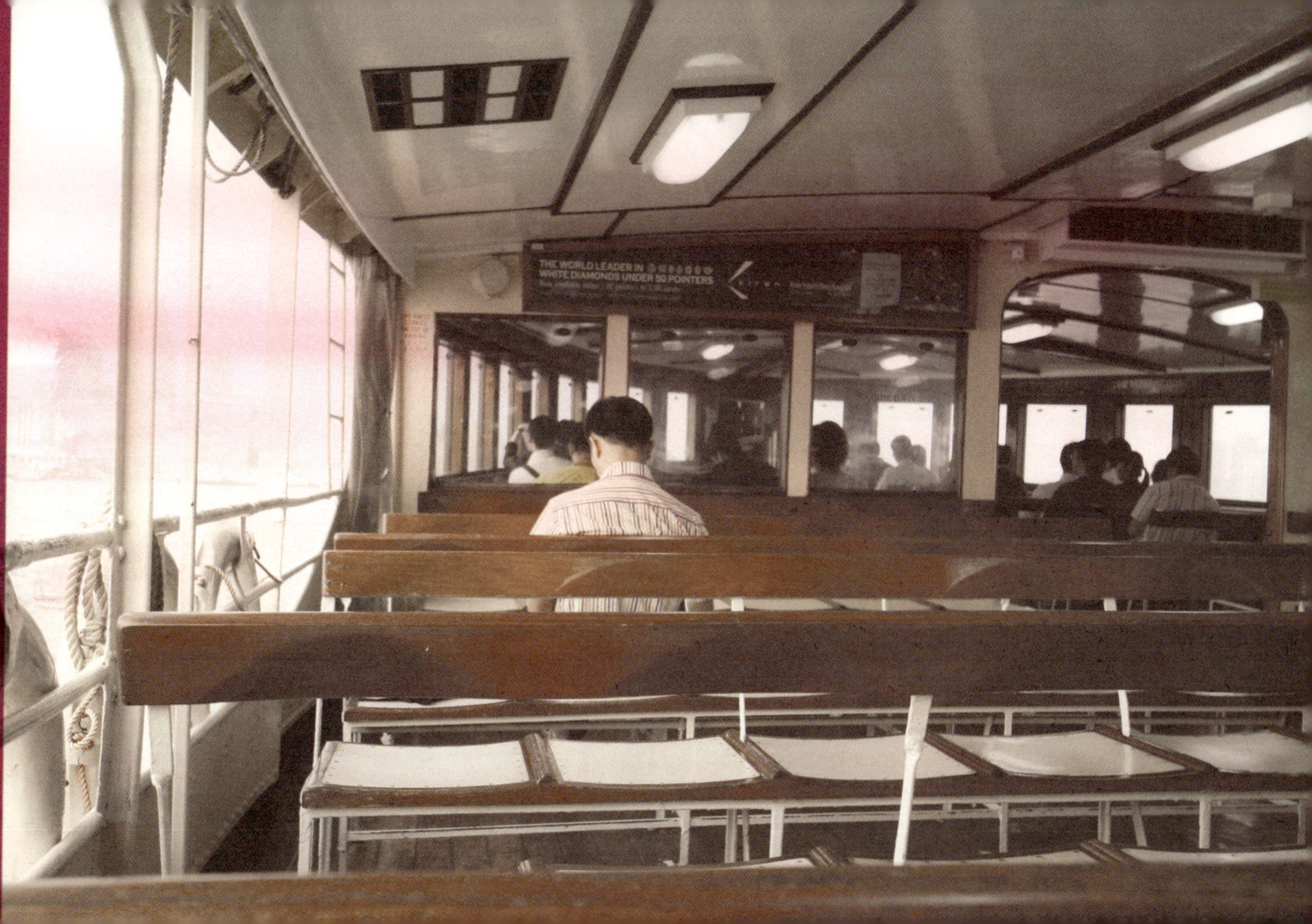
THE WORLD LEADER IN
WHITE DIAMONDS UNDER 50 POINTERS

Merge East and West in

WAN CHAI

Where the Middle Meets

We don't like our cities too tidy. We're the same way with neighbourhoods. We love local, messy, old, a bit disheveled and dirty. We also love new, modern, clean and comfortable. In Wan Chai, you get both: Beautiful boutiques and chaotic markets, heritage buildings revived into fine dining restaurants, bookstores and antiques, cafes and *cha chaan tengs* and of course, the grungier bits home to the historic red light district made infamous by Suzie Wong.

Wan Chai holds all of this — the old and new, young and aged, expats and locals, the rich and not-so-rich — beautifully in her arms. They're all here, co-existing in that quintessentially Hong Kong way without need for explanation, justification or even much celebration. Wander with us as we count the ways Wan Chai merges the mystical East with cool, modern West.

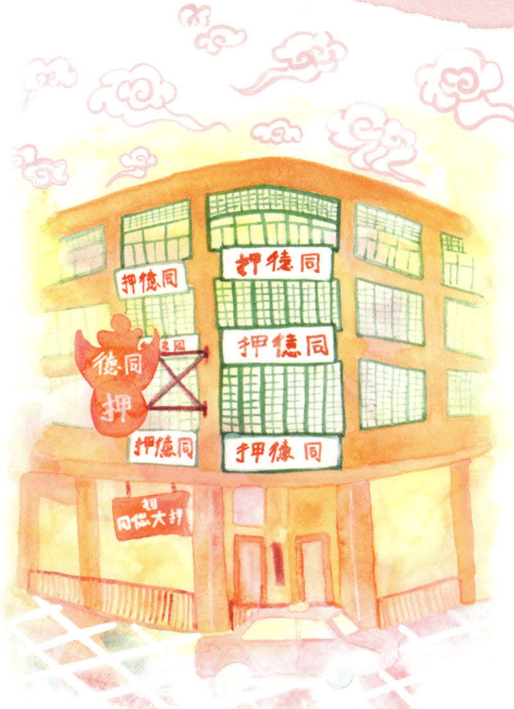

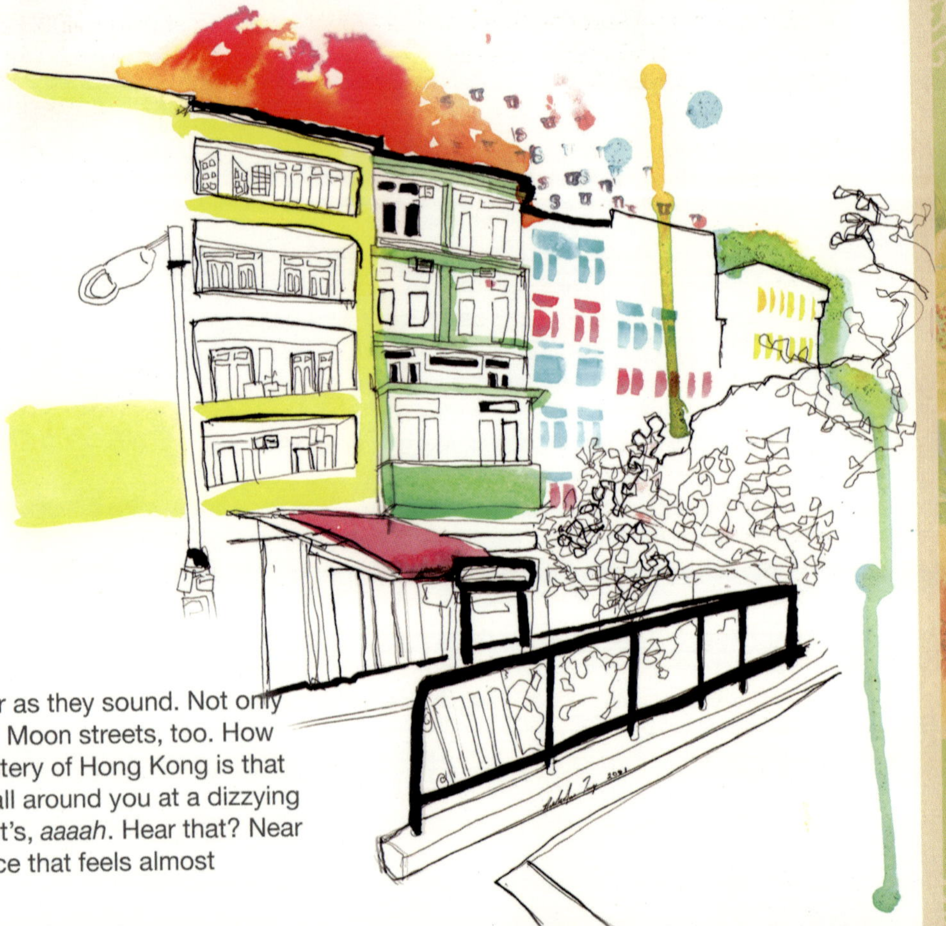

West

Star Street

These streets are as fun to wander as they sound. Not only is there a Star Street, but Sun and Moon streets, too. How romantic is that? The strange mystery of Hong Kong is that life mostly thunders and crashes all around you at a dizzying pace, then you turn a corner and it's, *aaaah*. Hear that? Near silence. And a sudden relaxed pace that feels almost European. That's Star Street.

So perhaps it's no surprise that it was a Frenchman who staked out this overlooked hilly corner, turning it into one of the city's more interesting micro-neighbourhoods. Arnault Castel moved to Hong Kong in 1996 as an investment banker but gave it up for a more personal enterprise in retail. In 2006 he opened Kapok, a beautifully curated lifestyle boutique in Tin Hau, before discovering this location in 2008 which was somehow both easy to reach and yet hidden away. It was our search for his little shop that first led us here, but it took a while to find. Where the heck was St. Francis Yard? We looked on the map, we asked locals. Nobody could figure it out. Everyone we asked, at the time at least, had never heard of the street. After much to-ing and fro-ing along busy Queen's Road East inhaling the fumes of double-decker buses, we finally found the narrow, steep street on the edge of Wan Chai that led us to his shop. We were delighted. And not just by Kapok (which still reigns as one of our favourite shops filled with small treasures from around the globe) but by the entire grid of slender streets flecked with eateries, art galleries and beautiful stores.

That these streets are named at all is something of a curiosity: Pedestrian-only Sun Street feels more like a forgotten alleyway sitting high above the hustle of Wan Chai with a grand banyan tree anchoring one end and a tall staircase leading back down to the city's noise on the other. Behind it are more lanes lined with cafes and boutiques alongside old warehouses and corner stores. Star Street holds a quiet sense of discovery and young, indie spirit that can be hard to grow in a city where rents are staggeringly high. And while we were slightly aghast to find that an American chain store had made its way here the last time we visited, this still feels like a secret between us and Wan Chai.

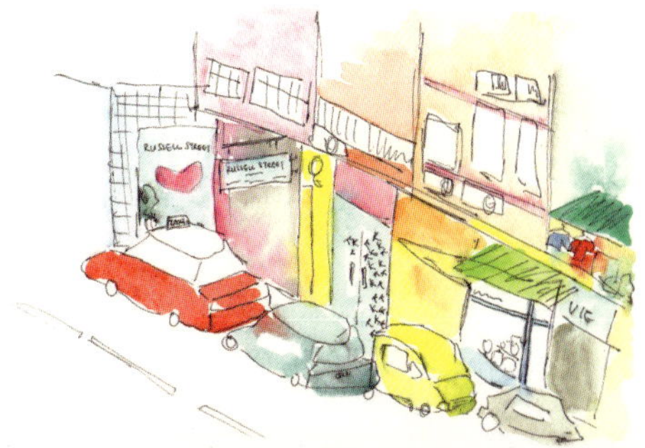

Street Markets *East*

If Star Street speaks to the arty hipster set then the markets of Wan Chai remind us that messy, scruffy street life is still alive and well. Each district of Hong Kong serves up a different flavour and its markets are the same way. Tai Yuen Street Market is the main one in Wan Chai, spilling over with cheap and colourful clothes, seasonal home decor trinkets, an umbrella stall that's been there forever and, if you were to ask Nick, the only reason to come here: Toys. (Did I mention my husband has an unhealthy addiction? He calls it a *collection.*)

Nick insists on stopping every time at Hung Hing Toys — you really can't miss it, it's right under the pink neon 'Underwear' sign. It's packed Tetris-style with Transformers, anime figures and, the last time I checked, tiny plastic Nike shoes in an array of colours (apparently another coveted *collector* item). I spend my time waiting outside, usually along with a few other parents while the kids (and Nick) rummage inside. To be fair, Nick is hardly the only adult in Hong Kong with a fondness for childhood paraphernalia. Here, it's absolutely acceptable for an adult to decorate one's car or home with plushies and plastic cartoon figures. For that reason alone (plus the fact that he's finally in a place where he's of average height) Nick feels unbelievably at home in this town.

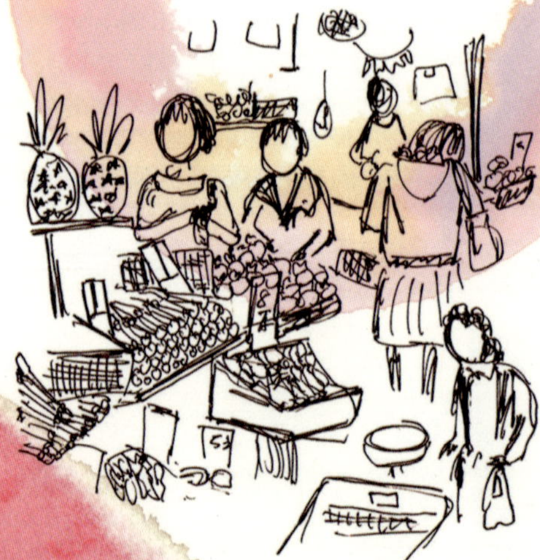

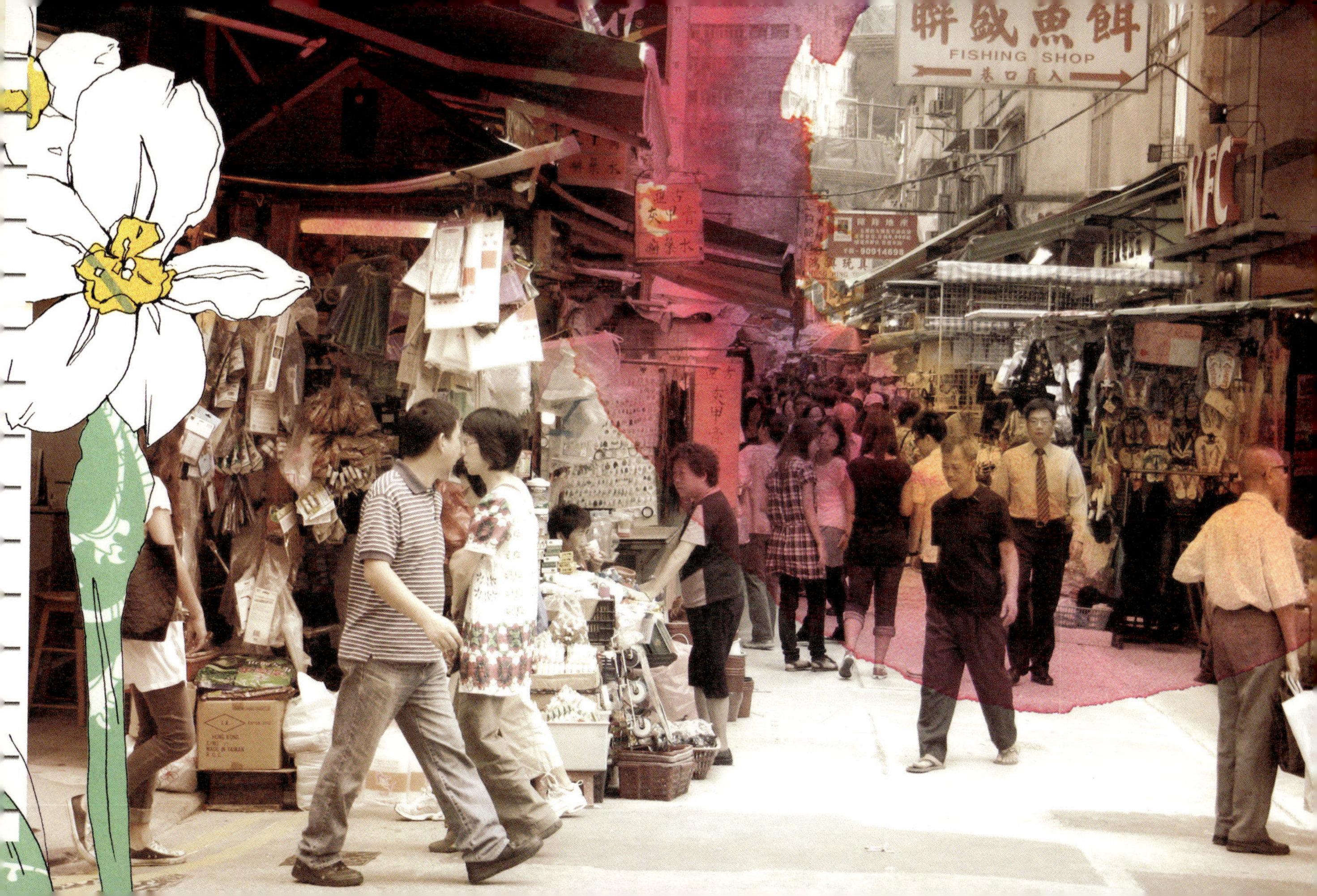
FISHING SHOP
巷口直入
KFC

The Traditional Bakery

East

Who wouldn't want to eat at the Happy Cake Shop? I hoped it'd be as good as it sounded. . . it was. What's more, the owner, Wong Hui Ping, is a curt but kindly man that I took a liking to right away.

Happy Cake Shop is a traditional Hong Kong bakery with its buns proffering a slightly sweet taste to suit the local palate. I love the pineapple buns* (a bestseller), which are always soft and comforting. Opened in 1979, with what look like the original yellow tiles still intact and blackened ancient stoves in the back, it's a piece of Hong Kong that reminds me of the simple pleasures of childhood. Nothing like a pineapple bun and Vitasoy milk to make me one happy camper!

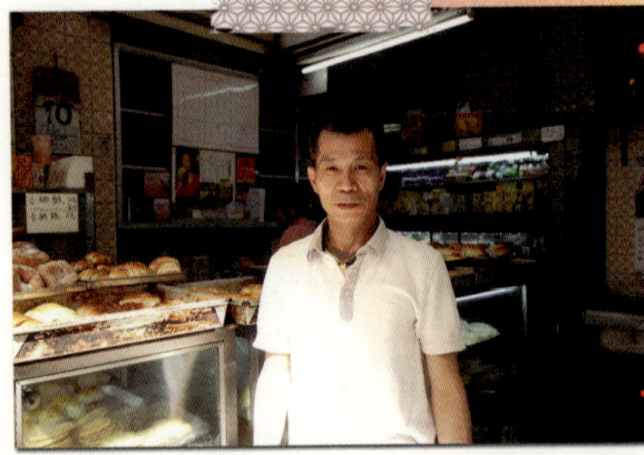

**Important note: A pineapple bun has never come into contact with an actual pineapple. A staple of the Hong Kong diet, this sweet bun is made with a buttery, crumbly topping patterned like the skin of its namesake fruit. Hence, pineapple bun.*

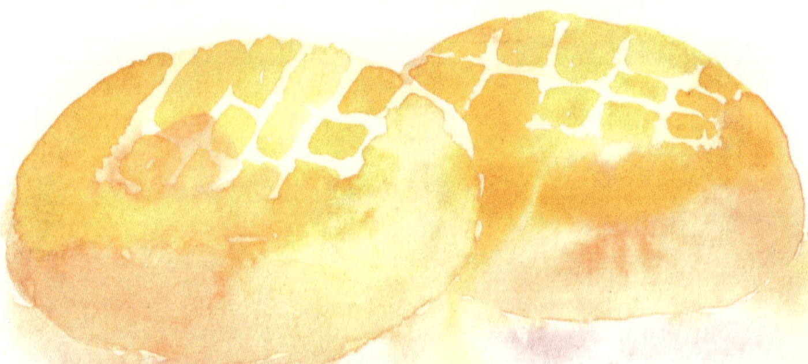

The Patisserie

West

When one is in the mood for something a little more sophisticated, there is always Sift, a sleek patisserie with scrumptious macarons. Lemon, caramel, raspberry and strawberry are just a few of our favourites. I'm pretty sure I had my first taste of macarons here when I stepped inside this glass box of a cake shop and got a bunch to go. We took our pretty box and headed to the grubby, concrete garden next door and Cookie Monster-ed the entire box in one sitting. It was a blissful, unfettered moment.

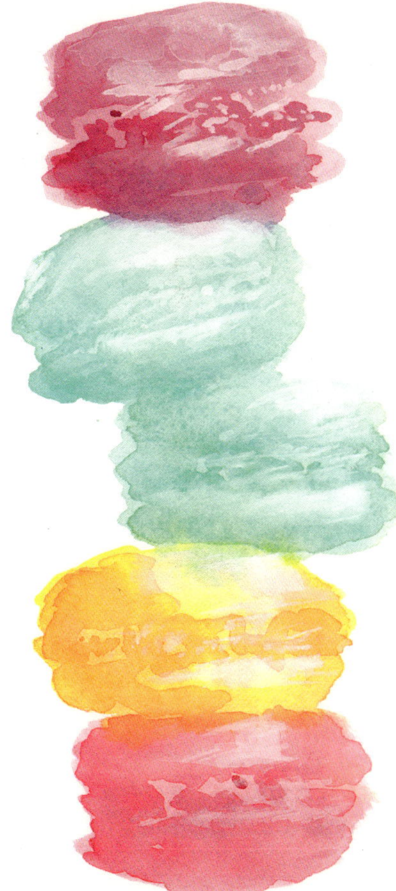

Slow Travel: Two Ways

We are definitely of the slow traveller variety. The kind who sits and looks, wanders and writes, sketches and paints while others keep to an itinerary of must-see monuments. Here are two ways to slow travel:

Photo safari

Hong Kong's full of buildings in various states of decay, but here they're really quite special. Go on a heritage photo safari and look out for the **Blue House**, revitalized tenements on **Mallory Street**, and the restored 20th-century shophouse on **Ship Street**.

Tip: Hong Kongers can be photo-shy and suspicious of photographers. OK, sometimes they can be downright cranky if they think a total stranger is taking a photo of them. A photojournalist friend with a knack for capturing wonderful candid shots offered these tips: Never try to hide the camera. Smile. If a stranger sees you, they'll either walk out of frame or, if they don't mind, they'll stay in frame. It's a nice touch, too, to show them the photo afterwards. Or, simply ask for permission — once I gathered the courage to approach strangers, I was surprised by how well this worked.

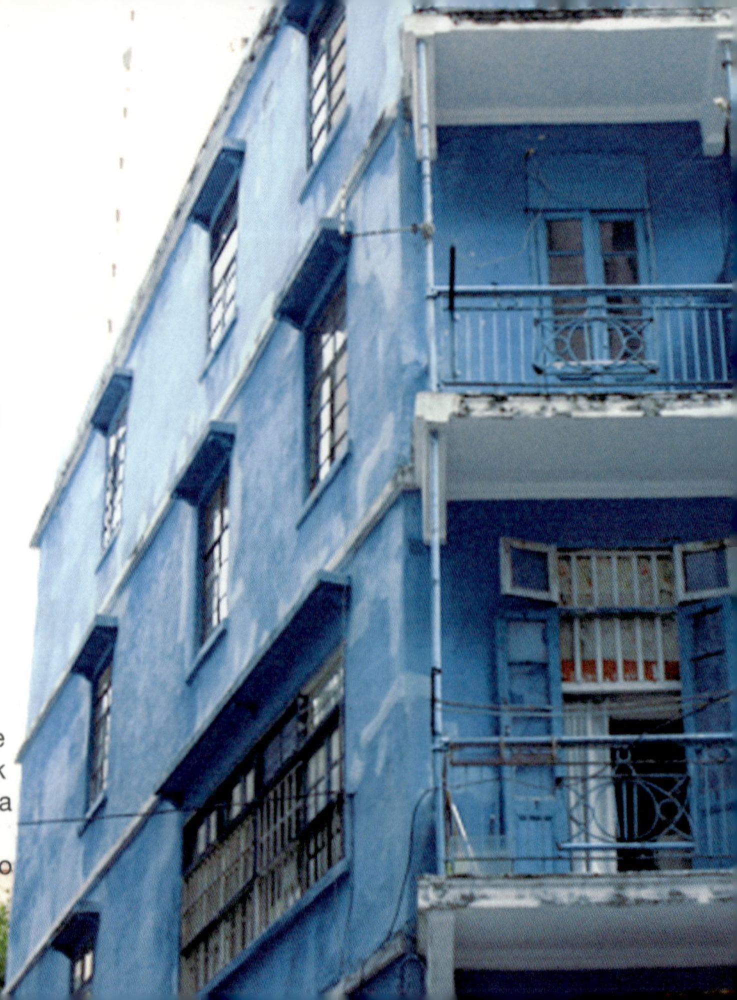

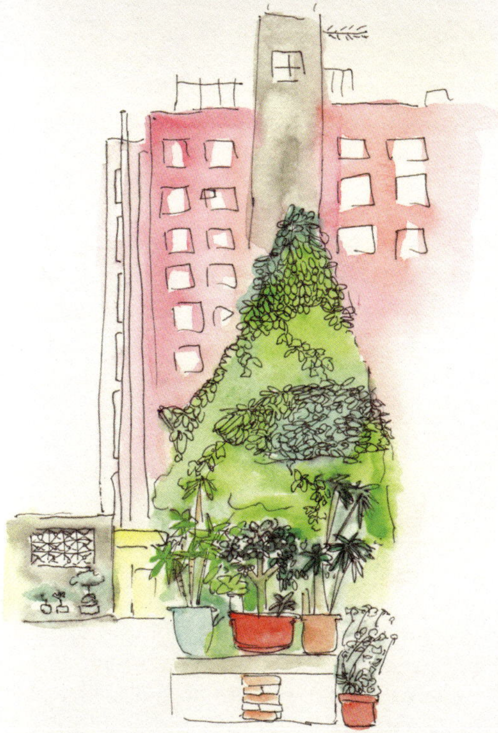

SAU WA FONG

Sketch the City

After breakfast with my cousin one morning, he asked what we were up to. Sketching, we said. He thought it bizarre, but it's one of our favourite ways to see the city. It slows you down enough to really notice the details. Pack a sketchbook, pencils, pens, watercolours, a bottle of water, paintbrushes and you're ready. Find a corner, draw and paint. It's one of the most satisfying ways to spend a few hours.

Blue House

In the fall of 2006, Hong Kong discovered a newfound passion. And it was, surprisingly, firmly rooted in the past. For such a forward-looking city, this was nothing short of revelatory.

The flashpoint came when the government announced its plan to relocate the beloved Star Ferry pier — long a symbol of the city's history and romance — in the name of land reclamation. Hong Kongers were incensed. In a city accustomed to demolition, its people finally found its limit — and discovered not everything old could be discarded so easily.

Despite widespread protests, the government rammed its plans through. But that event sparked a grassroots movement on preservation. As a result, places like the Blue House now had, for the first time, a fighting chance at survival.

The Blue House represents everything about old Hong Kong that's worth holding on to — and a lot that's not. Built in the 1920s as a residential tenement for the poor, the Blue House is a classic *tong lau*, a combination of Chinese and western architectural style particular to this region. It was common for a family of eight or 10 to rent a single bed and call it home. Old black-and-white photos show small rooms crammed with three-level bunk beds, each bed a "home" for a family. And if you needed to use the washroom, well, forget it. There were none. Everyone had to use the nearby public washroom, as Wan Chai resident and Blue House activist, Ah Wah, tells it.

Living in such tight quarters underscored the poverty of many Hong Kongers in the first half of the 20th century. But the house also symbolizes a simpler time: a deep sense of togetherness that many fear is being lost in modern-day living. "Why do we feel nostalgic? Honestly, it's not because of the buildings," says Ah Wah in Cantonese. "They really are very old, some of them are dangerous to live in and they do need to be refurbished. But in redevelopment the government hasn't considered how to allow the original residents to stay. We hope by talking about it, we can pass on to the next generation that we need to cherish our communities, our neighbours and understand that current redevelopment policies are affecting this greatly."

Thanks to the dedication of activists such as Ah Wah, four years of negotiation with the government to preserve Blue House brought results in 2010. Government plans to turn it into a schmaltzy tourist attraction were overturned in favour of renovating the derelict house, including outfitting it with much-needed washrooms and allowing its longtime residents to remain. The ground floor is now also home to the small and quirky Wan Chai Livelihood Museum, dedicated to educating the public about Blue House and Wan Chai's past. The fight, however, for preservation activists like Ah Wah is not necessarily over. All over Wan Chai, luxury residential properties are being erected, and the fear is that the Blue House will stand alone in its escape from the wrecking ball.

"People say if you don't tear down the old, how can you make way for the new? It's true, but I feel in this reconstruction you can achieve a balance," says Ah Wah.

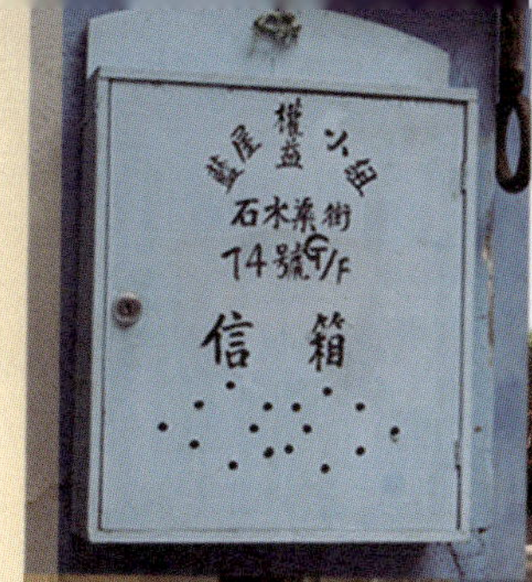

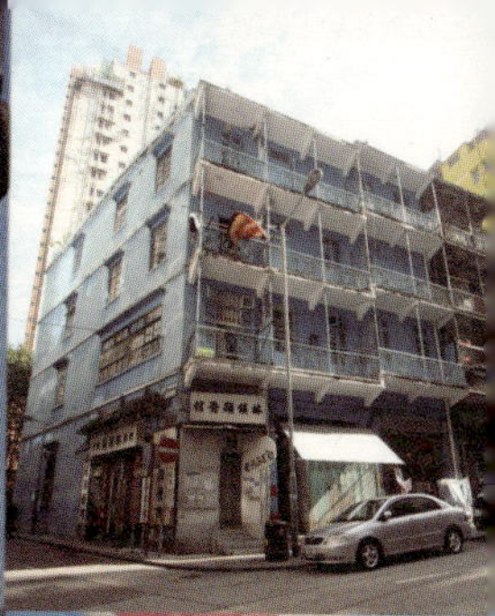
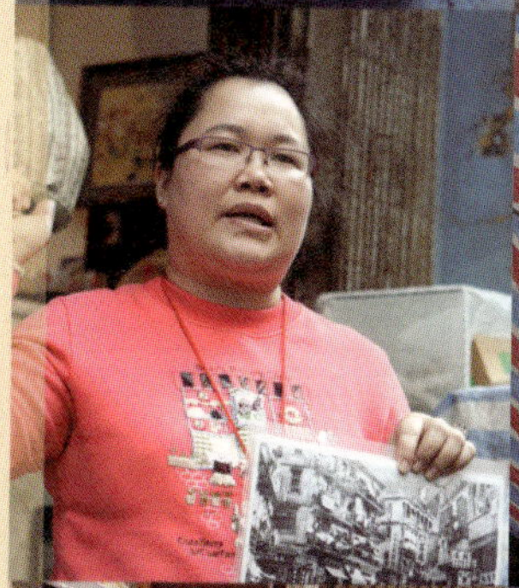
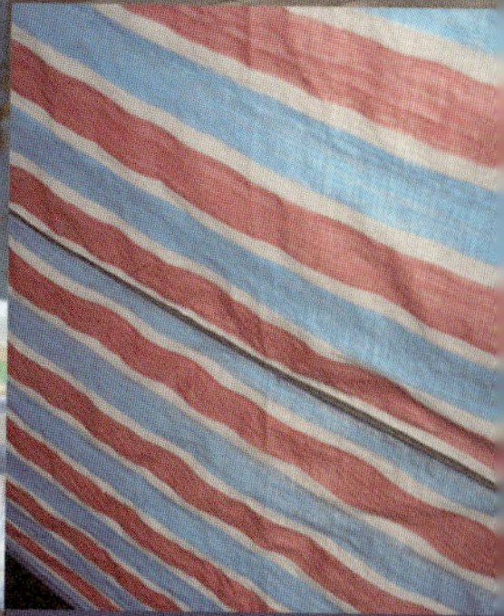
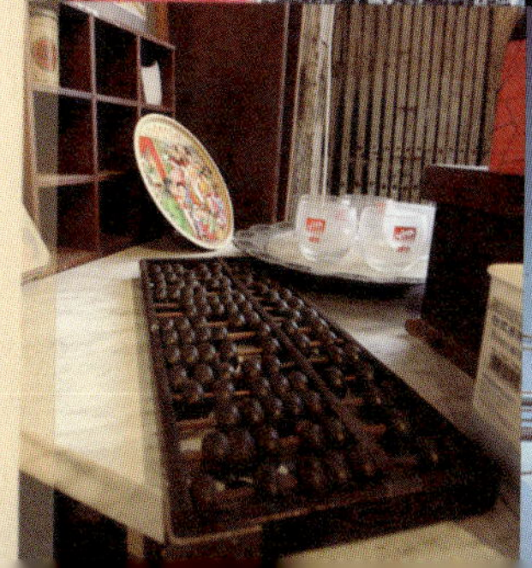
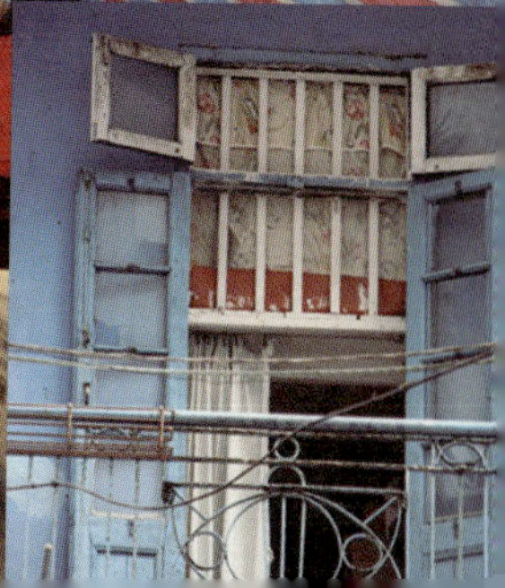

Behind Closed Doors

Sometimes it takes a tourist's curiosity to find the real gems in a city. So when our dear friends Kirk and Kathryn landed in Hong Kong, how could we not follow them — and their cute, hand-drawn map — to Ta Pantry, a reputedly delicious private kitchen?

For the uninitiated, private kitchens are semi-illegal, unlicensed restaurants in which locals open their private spaces to cook for strangers. Chef Tata greeted us at the door: Tall, pretty and slender, dressed in a pink chef's apron. She seemed just a tad nervous, which only endeared her to us more. A former model who grew up in the States, Chef Tata's small apartment was charming and stacked with bottles of wine (courtesy of her wine-buying brother, she explained). Her food was delicious, the taste of a rich and pillowy *foie gras tamago* still stored in my memory bank. So here's to Kirk and Kathryn, and all travellers whose open hearts and open minds lead us to special places tucked right underneath our noses.

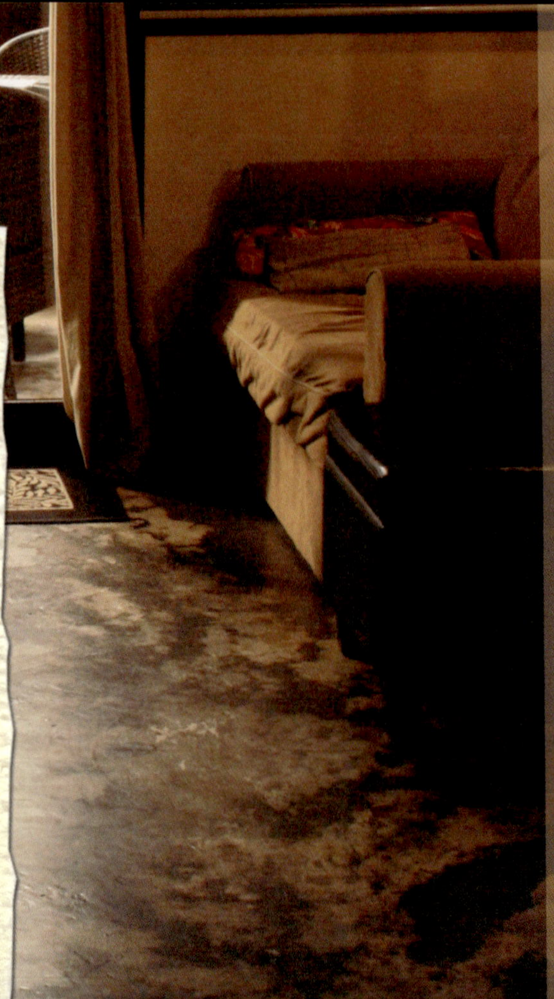

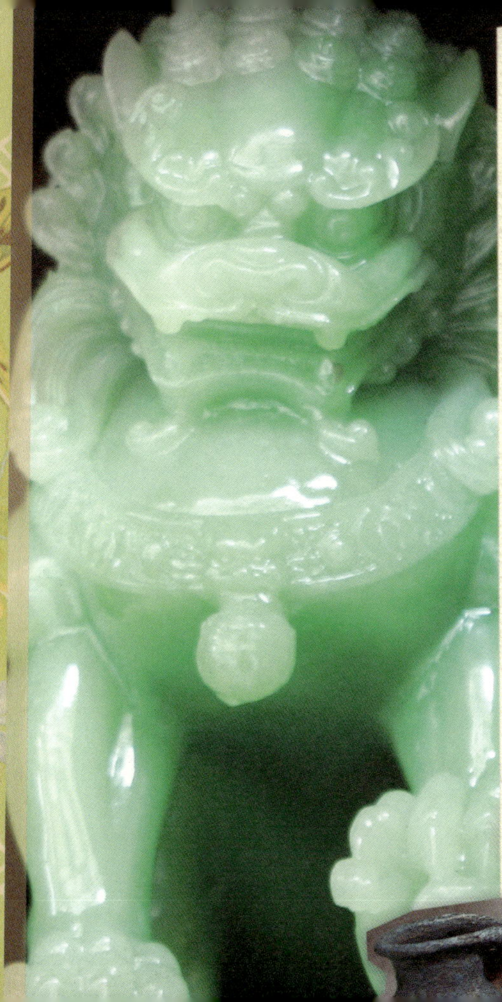

Out on the Street

He seemed a bit grumpy, but it was still early. Plus, reporters had made a habit of stopping by to ask nosy questions; I certainly wasn't the first. But Edward Chan humoured me anyway. The history of his exuberant shop in a nutshell: Necessitated by the need for a livelihood and inspired by travel, Chan decided to open a shop/stall filled with, by his estimation, roughly one thousand strange and wonderful objects from China and elsewhere in Asia. He curates by instinct. "Whatever I like," he says. His clients include serious *feng shui* practitioners in search of a particular rock, a ticking clock, or maybe a jade-carved lion. Then there are the tourists, expats and curious passers-by drawn to his marvellous collection of turquoise Foo dogs and bronze Hindu statues, all bursting forth onto the sidewalk from his teeny, tiny wonderland.

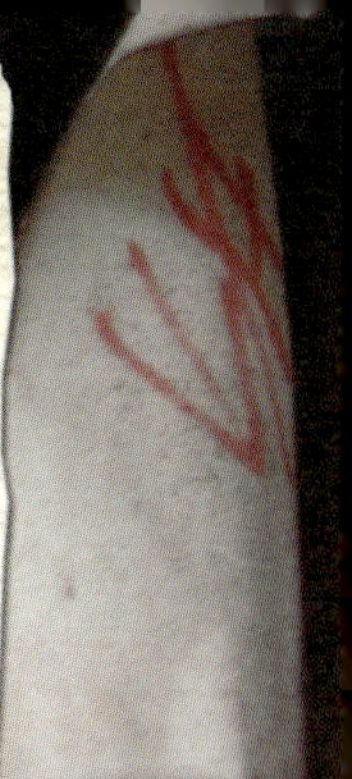

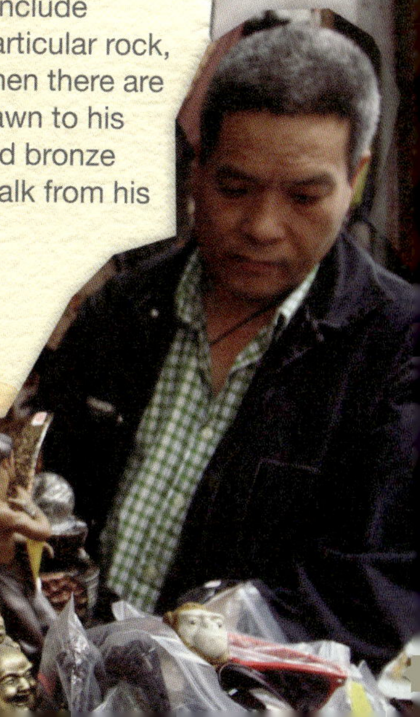

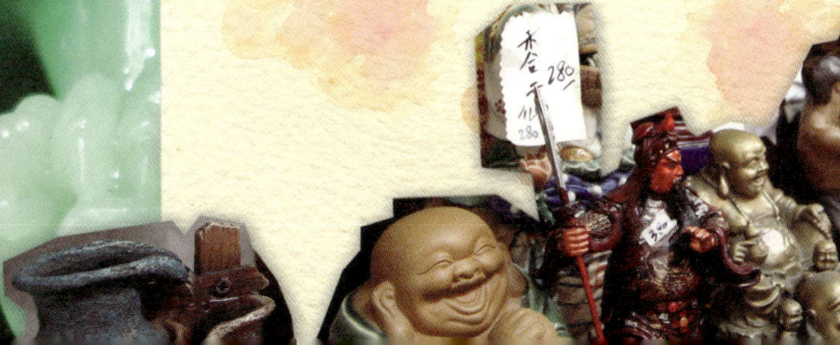

Remnants of a Colony

Every time we pass by The Pawn, we stop for a minute to admire its elegant lines — a throwback to the days when women sashayed in *cheongsams* and rickshaws clacked through the streets. There's something special about this gently curved building, a former pawn shop built in 1888, and it lived up to the promise of a surprise. Up the narrow set of stairs and The Pawn, now a restaurant, welcomed us with waiters in bow ties and quirky plaid pants. Divided into several rooms over three floors, the dark, colonial-meets-Chinese interior was the work of Hong Kong art star anothermountainman (Stanley Wong).

The bar featured deep, vintage leather sofas and Chinese pawn shop bills for art; upstairs in the restaurant area were wooden tables and locally-designed wallpaper panels. Whirring fans hung above the generous balcony. The Libra in me loves a beautiful room and this it was. Wong described it as a Hong Kong version of a British gastropub. Which reminds me of the food. I admit I wasn't sure about the British menu given the Chinese-ness of the *tong lau*, but then, what could be more Hong Kong than this mash-up of East and West? In the end, it was about the experience, which we loved through and through. We haven't visited The Pawn since it was renovated in 2014, which both surprised

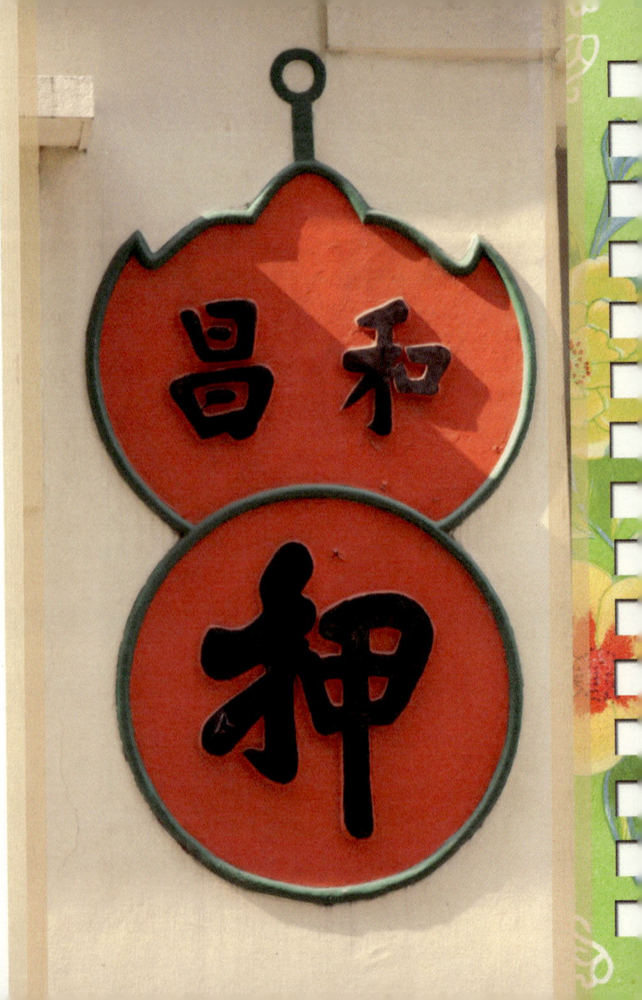

and saddened me a little. Tearing down those beautiful rooms? But then, what could be more Hong Kong than the continual stripping down and rebuilding up of the landscape? I imagine this beautiful old building has many more reincarnations left in it yet.

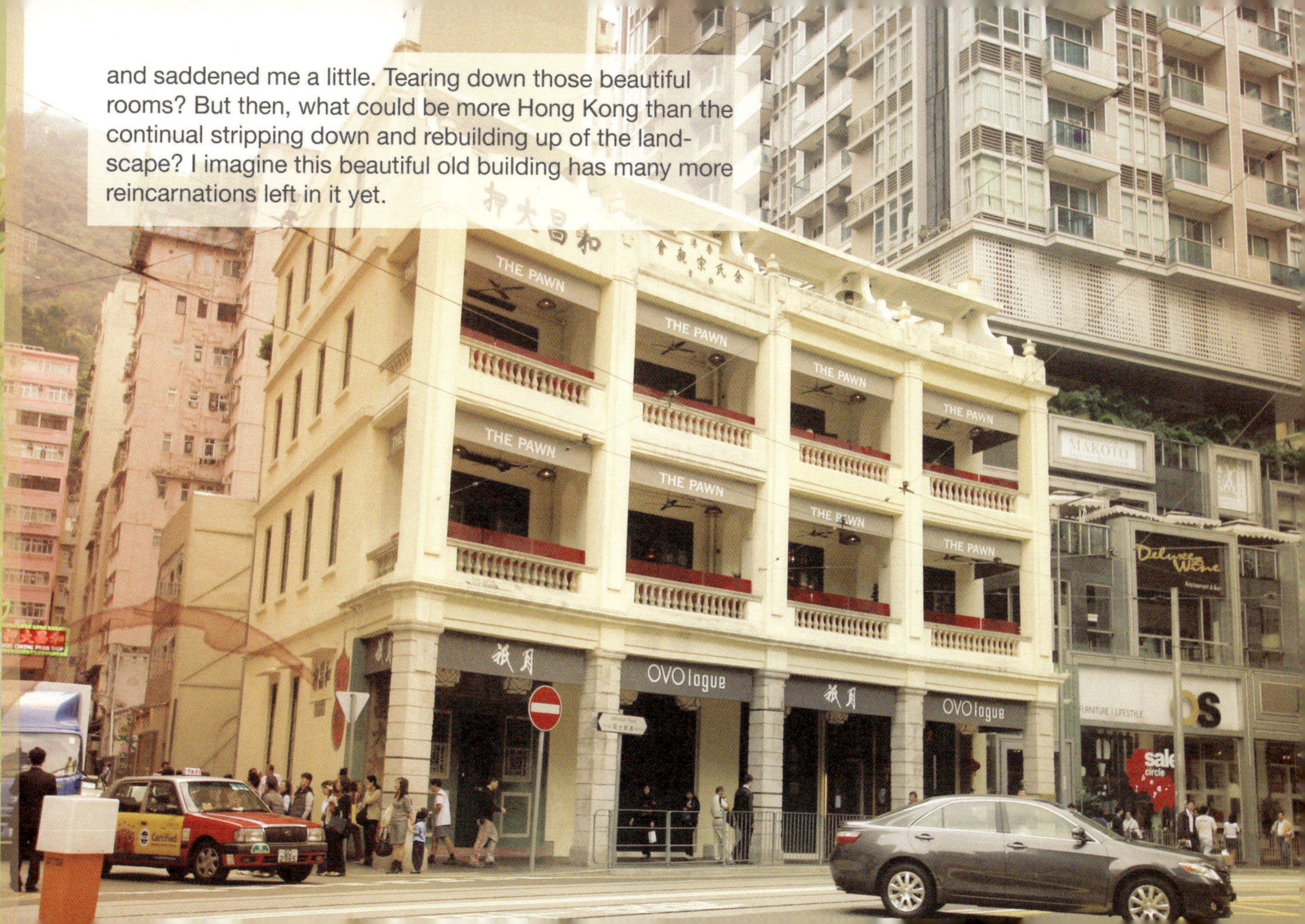

SHOP TILL YOU DROP IN

CAUSEWAY BAY

Renting Happiness

Whoever said you can't buy happiness forgot to mention that you can rent it, however temporarily. And that, on some days, is good enough.

No, shopping can't fix that job you hate, or the broken heart you're nursing. But it sure can make it a lot more palatable. Hong Kongers believe in the power of shopping. Yes sirree. I have spent many a day shopping in this city (really, how could you not?). To assuage my consumerist guilt, I save most of my shopping for our annual trips to Hong Kong, where buying things is virtually irresistible. As Nick likes to say, if there's a square inch available, someone will be selling something on it. Even on days when my sanctimonious self is lecturing that materialism is no way to happiness, once I find myself in the swing of things, I am suddenly there: Totally present among the racks of clothing, vast array of shoes, and hey, is that a sale sign? It shouldn't be this fun, but as they say, to each one's own. Nick marvels at the way a bit of shopping and air conditioning can cheer me. Even when I don't actually buy anything — although let's face it, it's a lot more fun when I do.

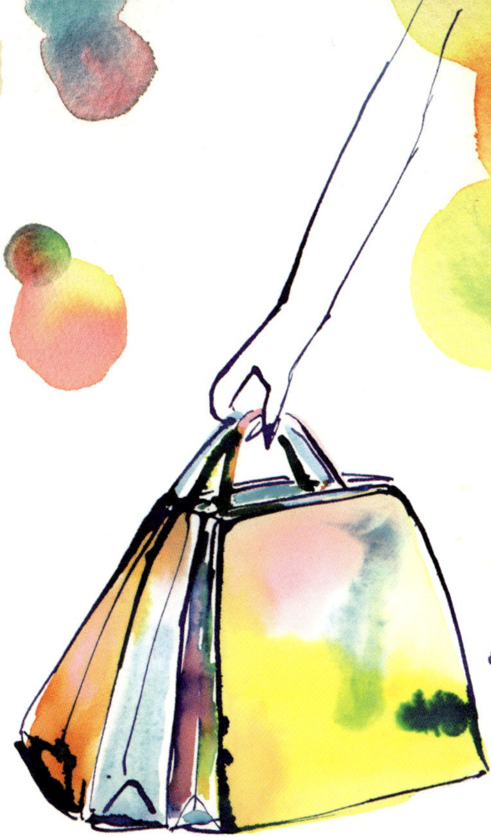

Committed to Fashion

This is what you need to know about fashion in Hong Kong: It's all about commitment. Whatever a Hong Konger decides to wear, it's worn with an overzealousness rarely seen in other parts of the world. There's nothing self-conscious about it, it's never half-measured. It is always 100 per cent, full-on engagement.

It must be something in our blood. Chinese style has varied widely through the ages, but for the most part we have always loved bold, bright, clashing hues. And that's pretty much how Hong Kongers approach fashion. They don't want any old pair of jeans — they want it bedazzled on top of an acid wash. And if you're going to wear cow print, well, why not wear it from head to toe? (Fact: We once saw a very pretty girl dressed in cow-print shorts, cow-print hoodie and cow-print hat. She even had cow-print shoe-laces. It was phenomenal.) Or, if you love thigh-high leather boots and happen to be of a certain age — say in your 60s — why let that stop you? That's the attitude around here. If you're gonna wear it, go all the way. Mean it! Own it! One day, I intend to try this for myself. But until I find the courage to do so, I can only imagine the liberation that comes from dressing with such wild abandon.

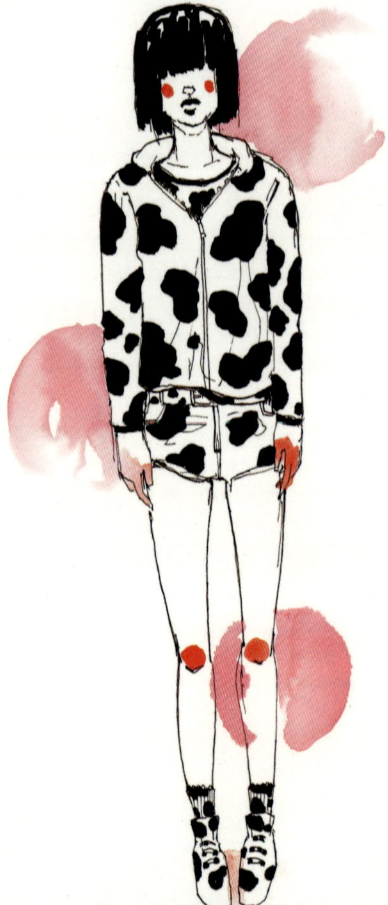

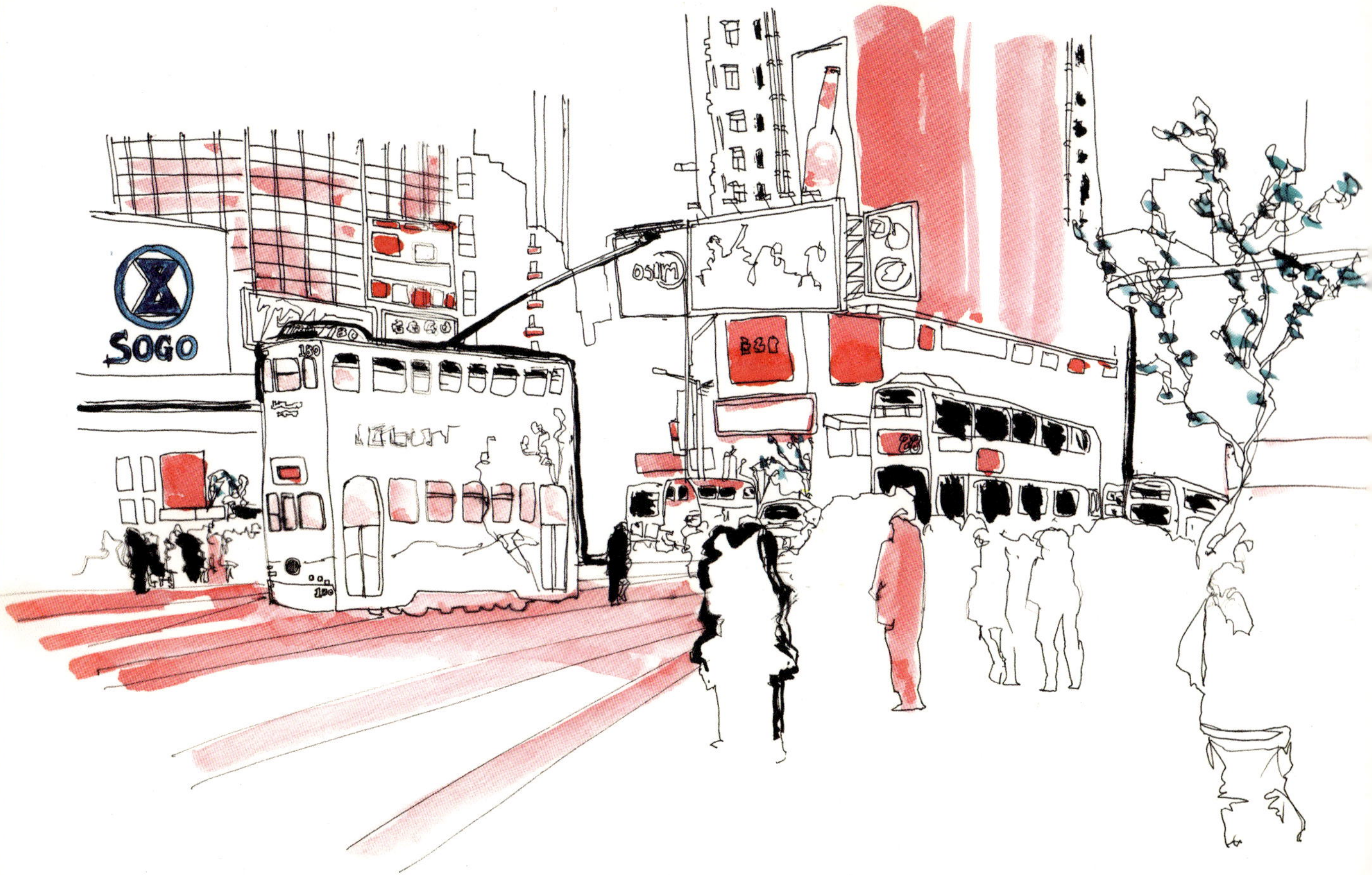
SOGO

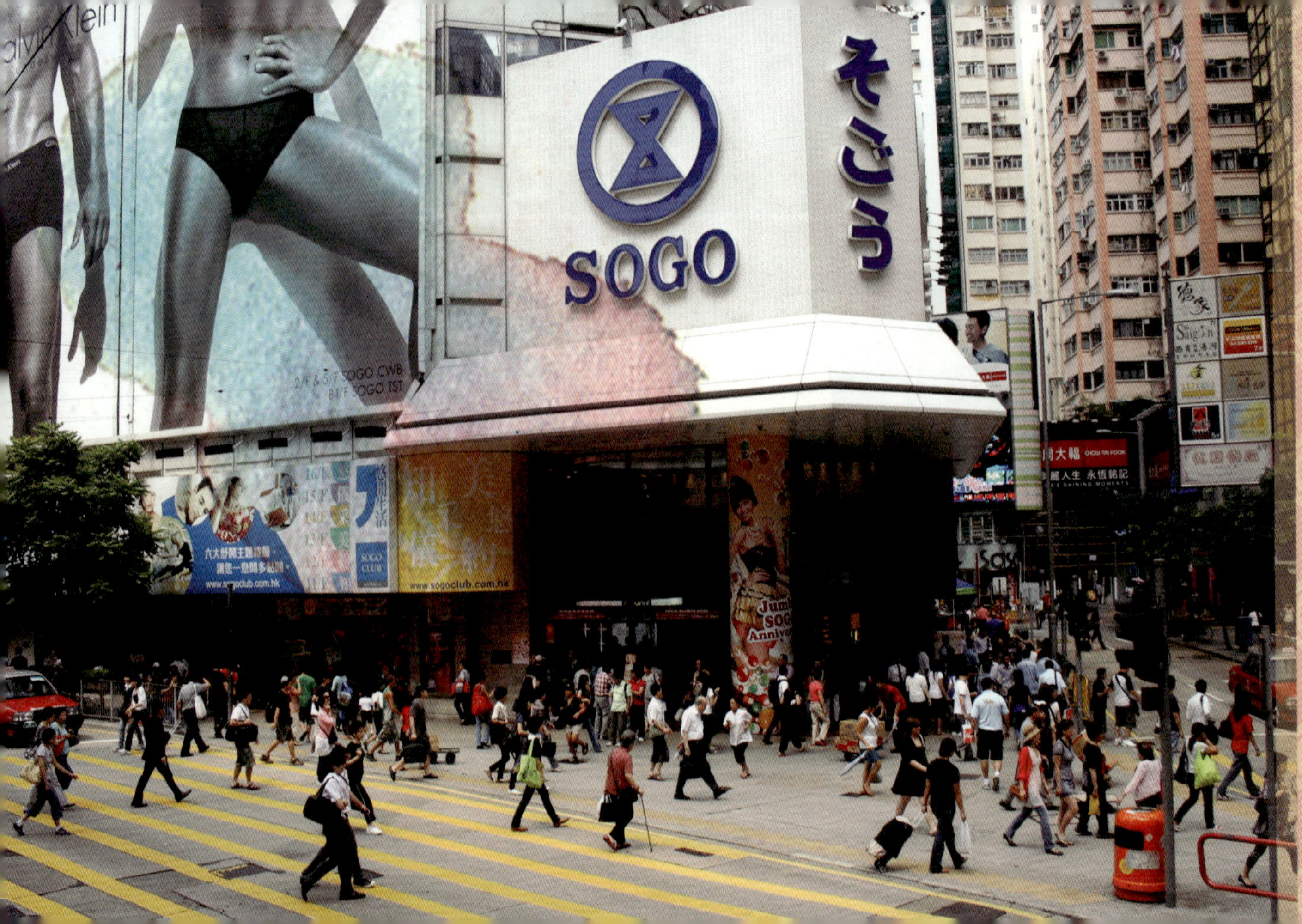
SOGO
そごう
2/F & 5/F SOGO CWB
B1/F SOGO TST
SOGO CLUB
www.sogoclub.com.hk
CHOW TAI FOOK

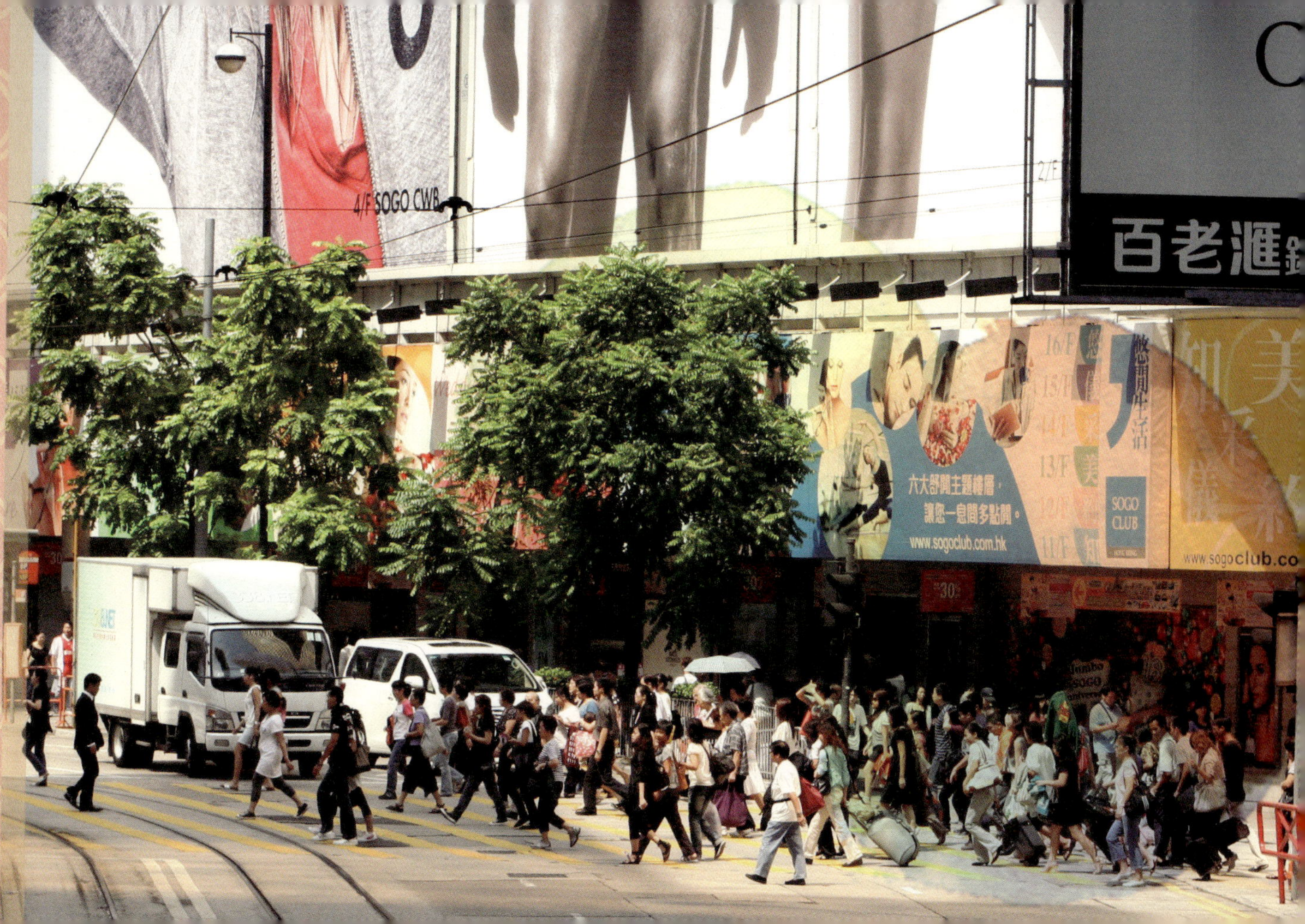
4/F SOGO CWB
百老滙
悠閒生活
六大舒閒主題樓層，
讓您一息間多點閒。
www.sogoclub.com.hk
SOGO CLUB

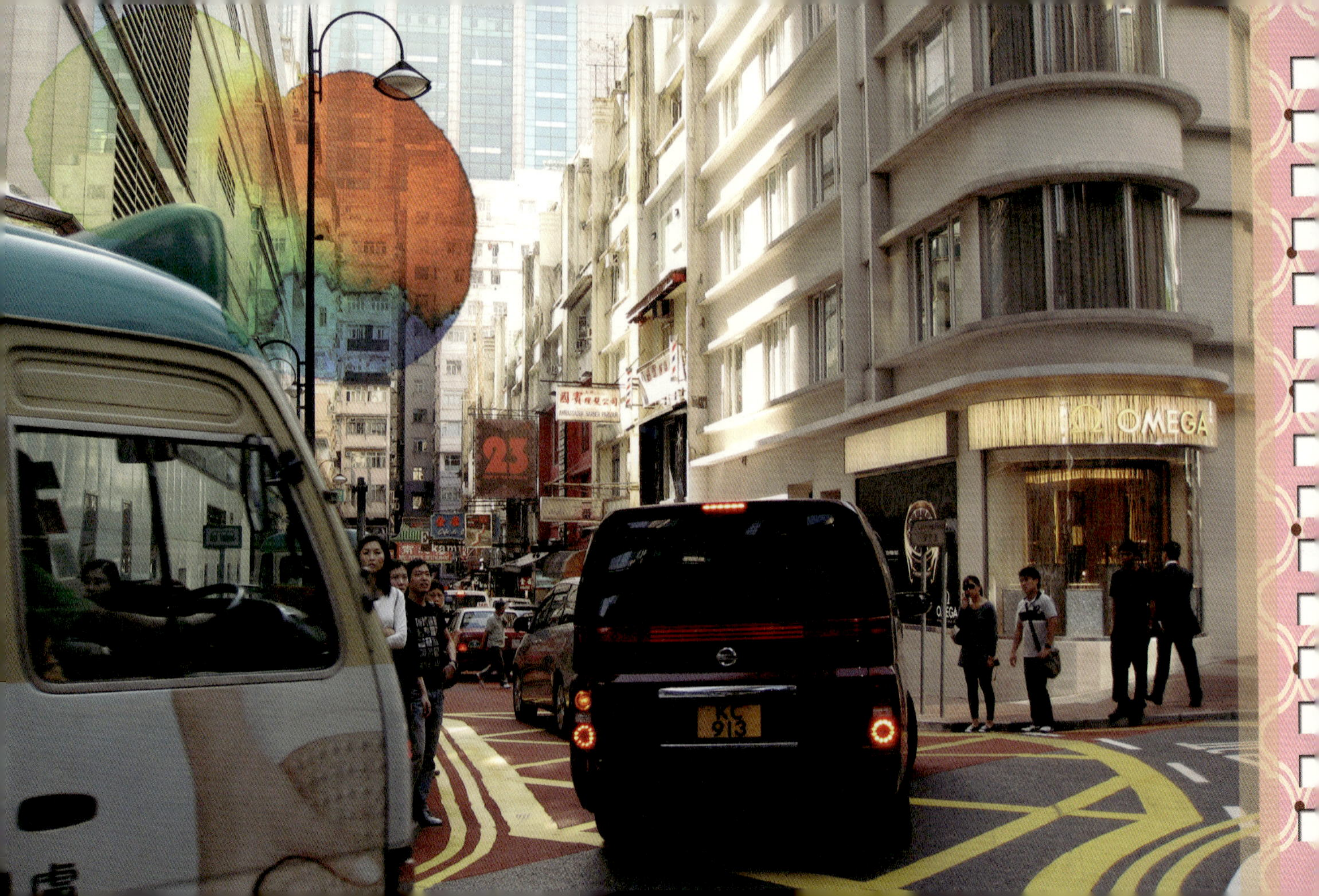
OMEGA
23

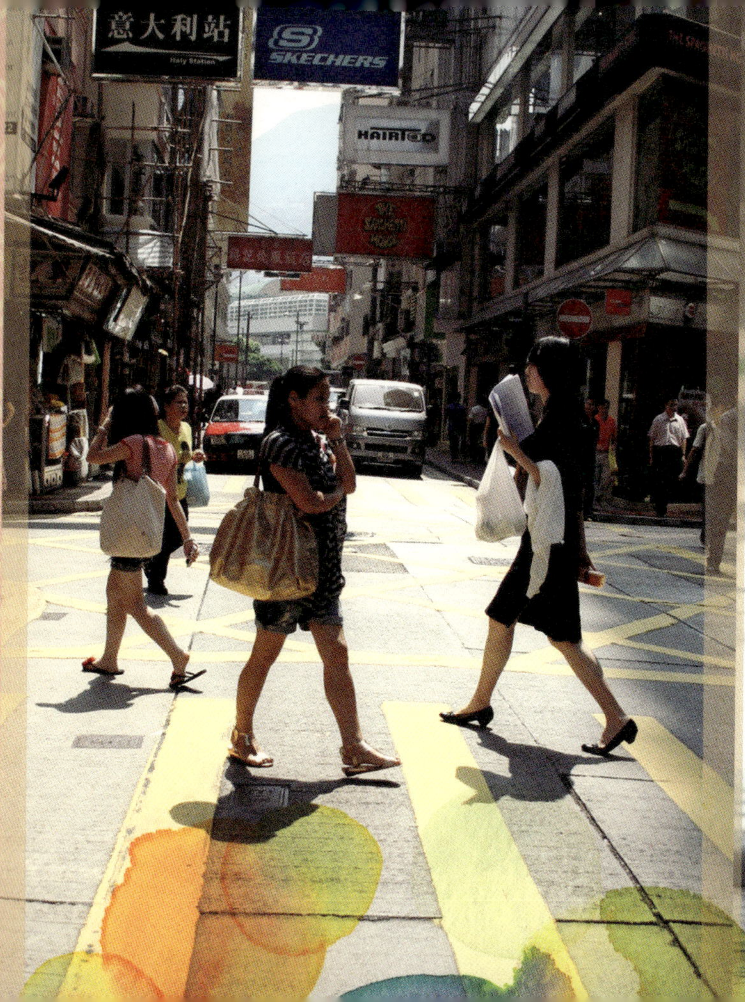
意大利站
Italy Station
SKECHERS
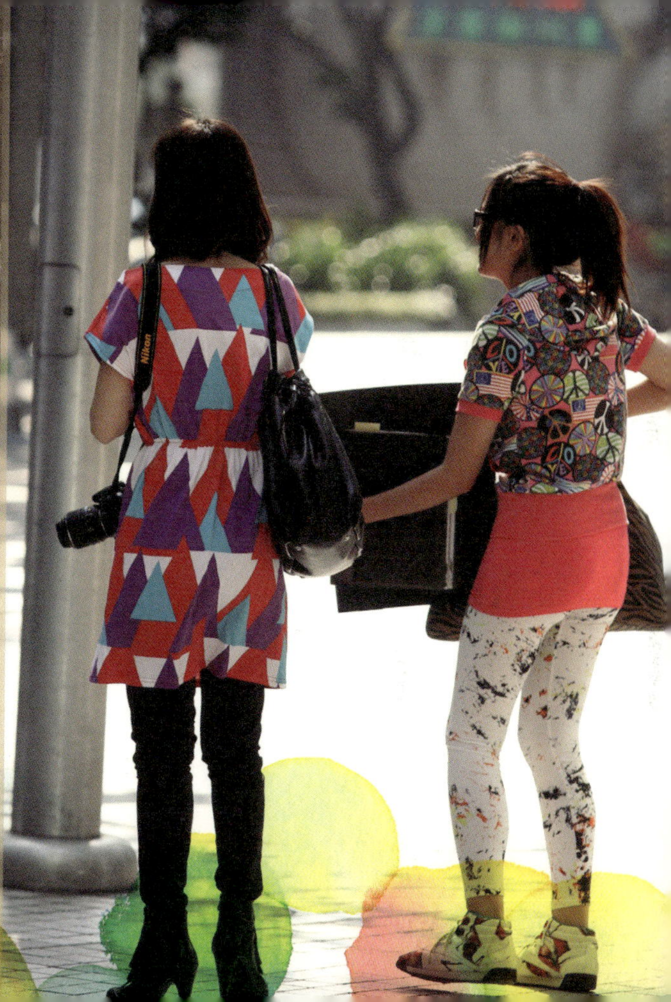

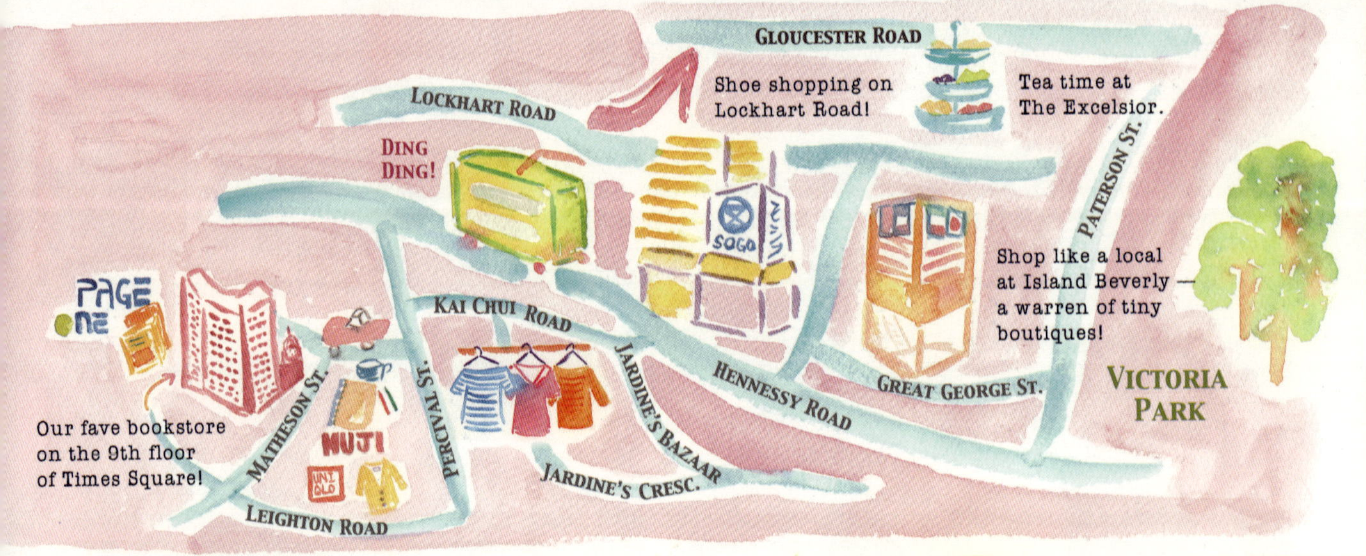

Treasure Hunting

Shopping in Hong Kong is a wild card. You cannot judge a shop by its cover, by which I mean, you can neither judge it by its name nor appearance. I have bought things I loved in a store chock-full of things I hated. I have bought things from boutiques with ridiculous names (like Dazzle Spirea, for instance). In short, it's a treasure hunt. It's a fun game. Just don't do it on Saturdays and Sundays when the rest of the city has gone treasure hunting, too.

My mom once split her wardrobe into two categories. One for when she visited me in Vancouver, another for home in Hong Kong.

VANCOUVER

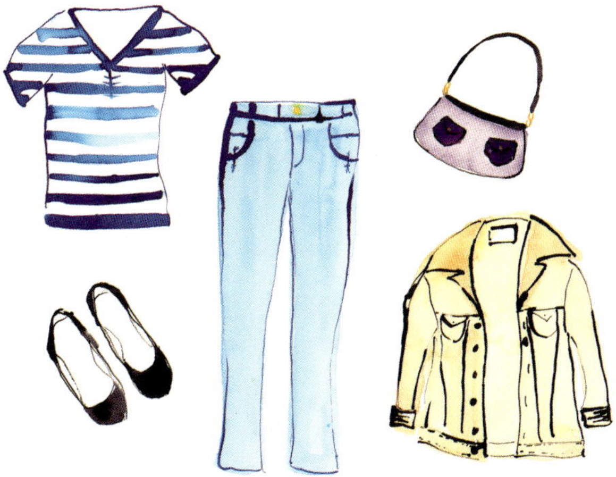

A practical ensemble that included classic striped tees, play-it-straight blue jeans, sensible jackets and tasteful black flats. All these adjectives are clearly synonyms in her mind for "boring."

HONG KONG

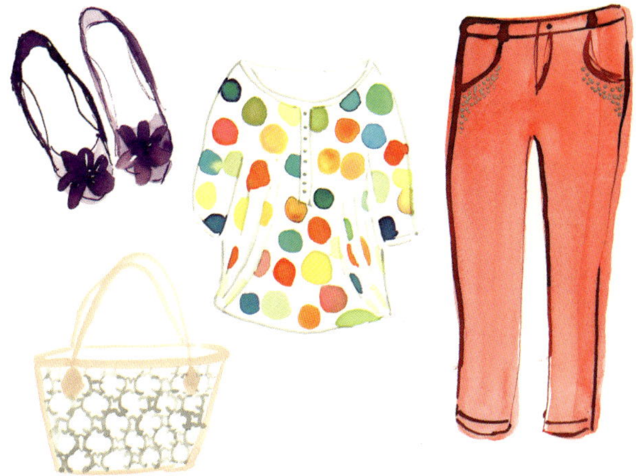

An interesting crop of tastefully cut jeans with a splash of sparkling insanity, an elegantly cut top with a flourish of polka dots you could spot from space, and of course, shoes painted a blazing neon. "Ho sharp!" would be her description of this wardrobe.

The Haul

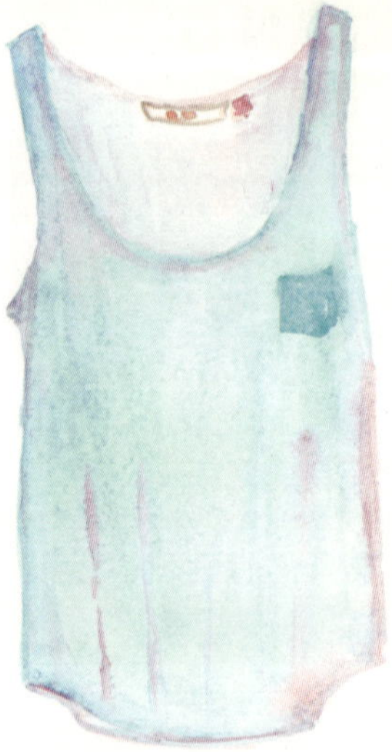

The perfect tank: Not too loose, not too tight. Bought in cream, black and turquoise.

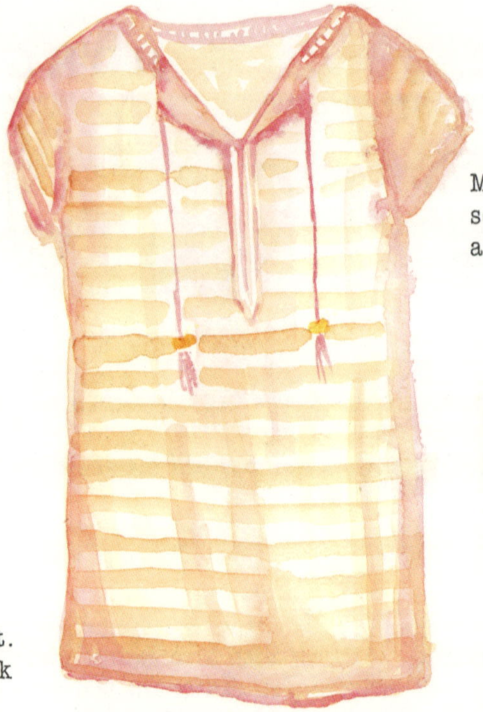

Gauzy tunic dress, perfect for hot summer days.

Maxi skirt for schlepping around at home.

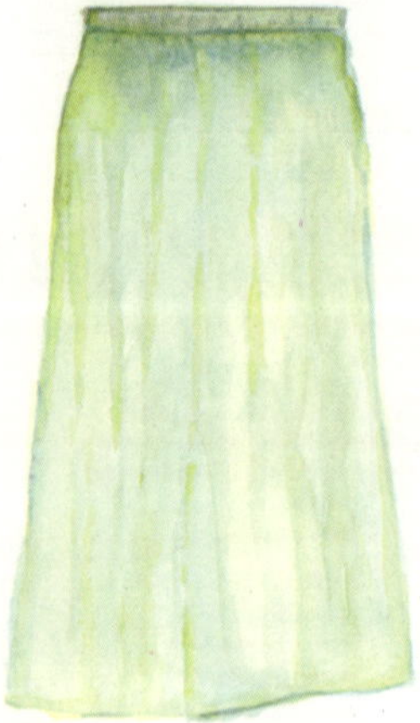

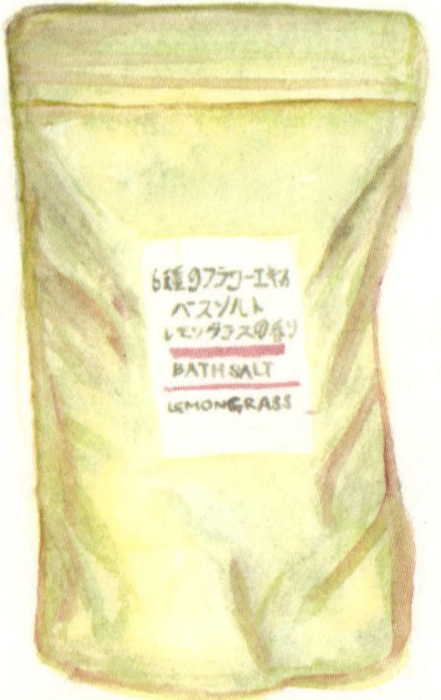

Muji bath salts for cold winter days back home in Vancouver.

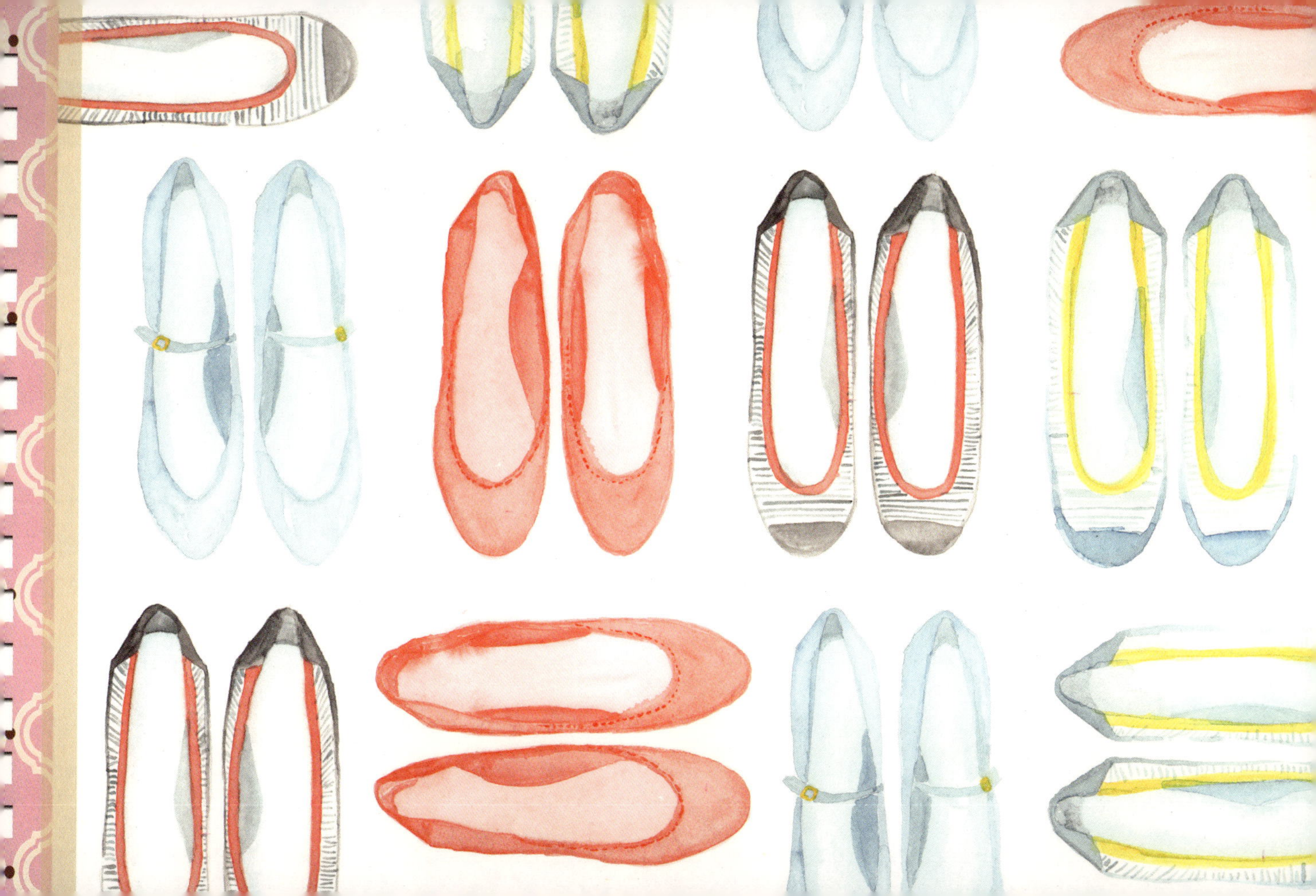

Hung Hing Tea

On the cold dark days of Vancouver, when the buzz of Hong Kong seems very far away, I have enjoyed many a cup of *cha* bought from this ramshackle of an old tea shop, which always reminds me of my travels home.

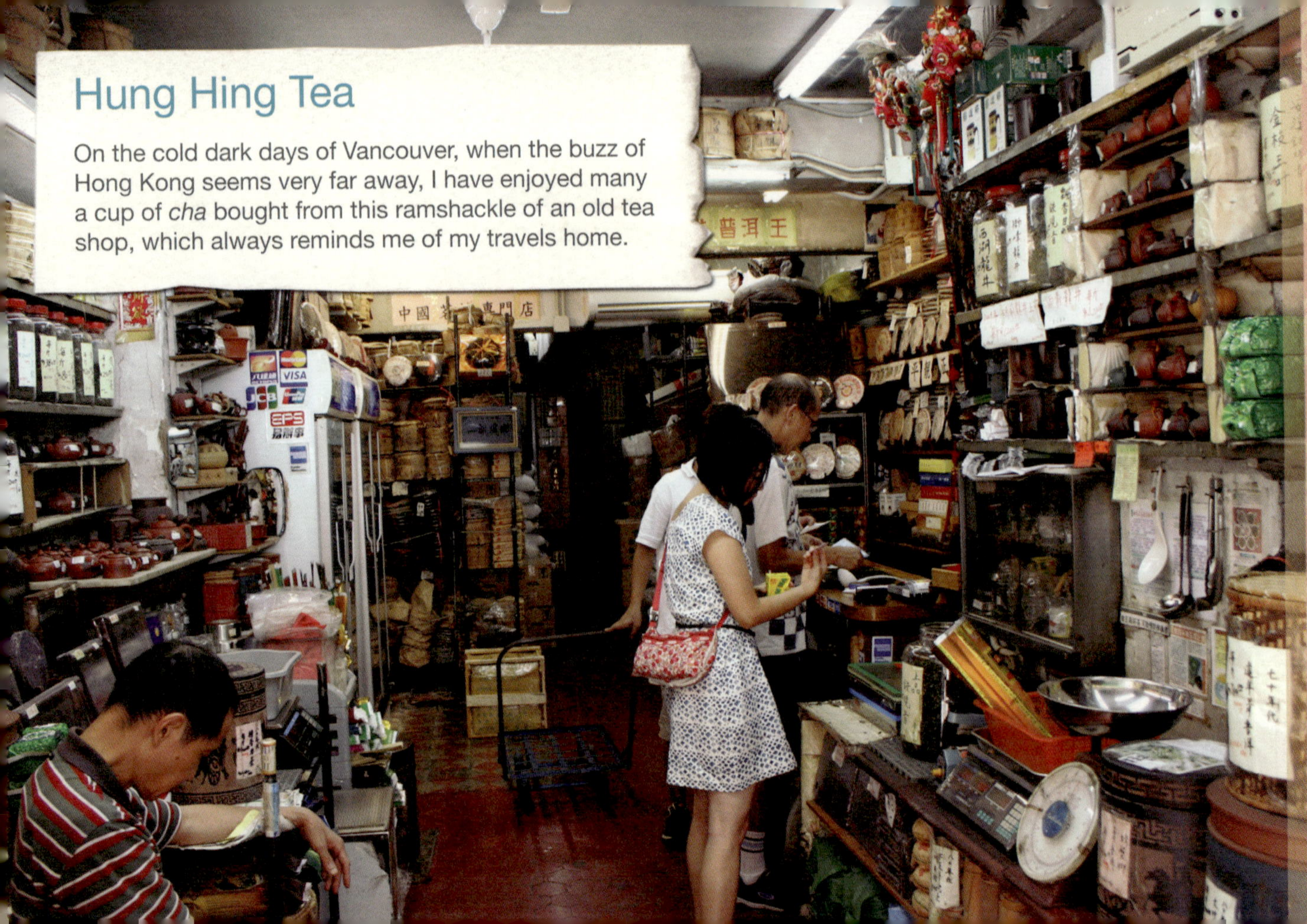

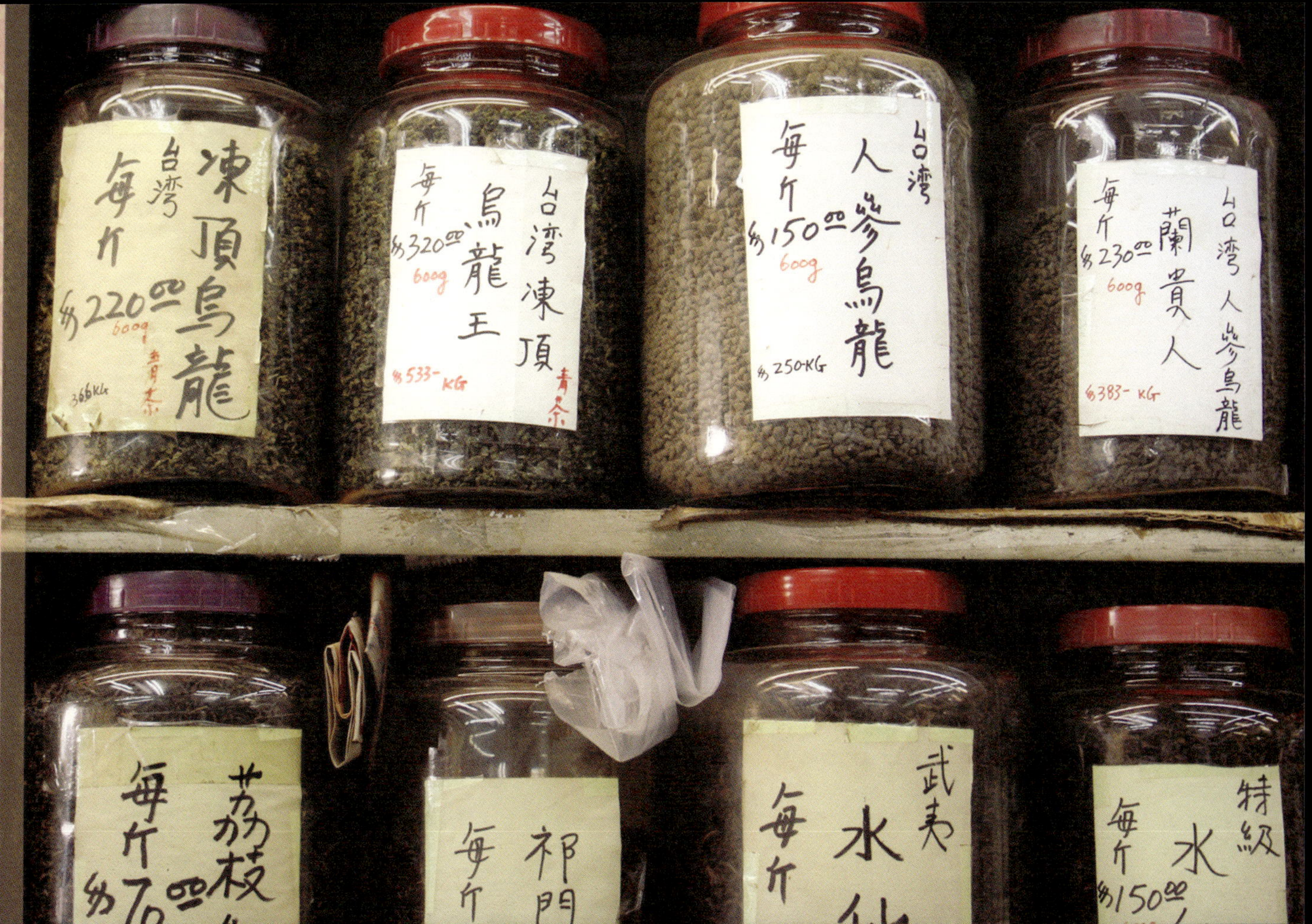
台湾
凍頂烏龍
每斤
$220
600g
366KG
青茶
台湾凍頂
烏龍王
每斤
$320
600g
$533-KG
青茶
台湾
人參烏龍
每斤
$150
600g
$250-KG
台湾人參烏龍
蘭貴人
每斤
$230
600g
$383-KG
每斤
每斤
武夷
每斤
特級
每斤

Little Red Bookstore

It seemed apt that we found ourselves at the People's Recreation Community Bookstore and Cafe on the 60th anniversary of the People's Republic of China. For days, the news focused on nothing but Chinese patriotism — and not just the manufactured kind indoctrinated by the powers-that-be in Beijing. This was the 21st century after all, China's century, and the pride of the people could be genuinely felt throughout the land.

But after a morning of watching Beijing parade its human and military might on TV, we were ready for a wander out. Remarkably, we found ourselves in what could only be described as a tiny but patriotic bookstore in the heart of Causeway Bay.

Running an independent bookshop in a city famous for its aversion to reading is no easy feat. That proved to be no exception for People's Recreation Community, which opened its doors in 2002 offering titles solely about mainland China. Subjects ran the gamut from travel to culture to politics — but it was the books banned in China that garnered the most attention. While locals showed little interest, word slowly trickled to mainland Chinese tourists that this was *the* place to find "sensitive" material, from

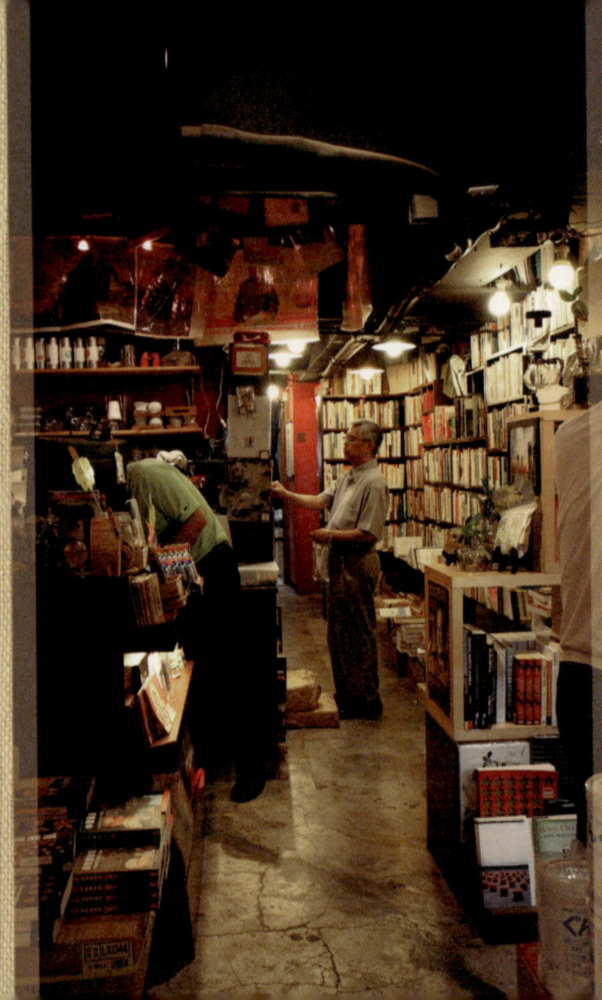

titles containing lurid details of political corruption to biographies of Mao Zedong. And for those of us who can't read a single word of Chinese, People's Recreation is simply a lovely celebration of Chinese writers and a quiet, hidden corner to escape the crowds.

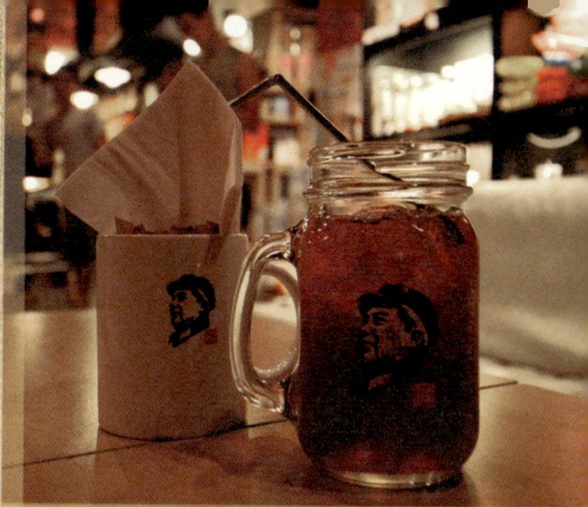

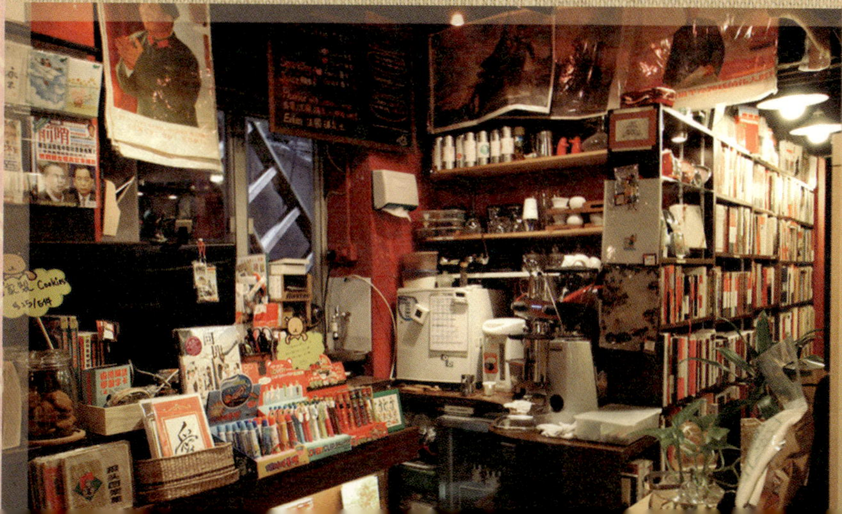

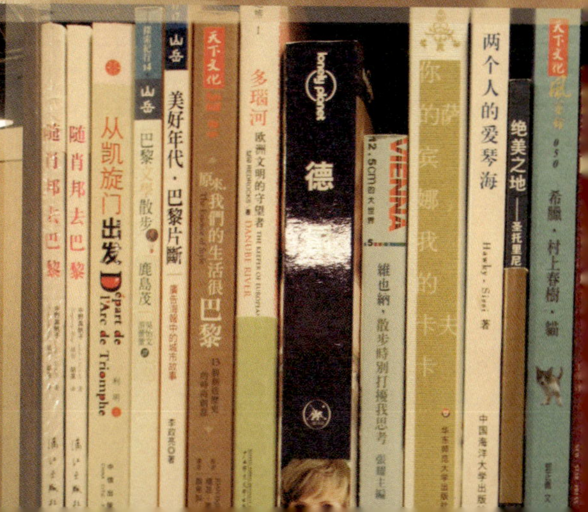

Daydream Nation

Daydream Nation is a Hong Kong fashion label created by brother-and-sister team Jing and Kay Wong. Each season Jing and Kay transport us to a world of play and whimsy. The siblings studied at Central Saint Martins in London but returned to their native city to start their own fashion label in 2006. Ever since then, they've garnered a steady following, including us! We sat down with Jing (who also happens to be a singer/songwriter) to find out more about what inspires their world.

We love the sense of whimsy behind Daydream Nation and we're curious about how it all started.
Well, it was always Kay's dream to be a fashion designer with her own label. But I'm actually more of a theatre person because I did theatre design and theatre directing — I've actually got a Masters in Theatre Directing. To me, when I first entered fashion, I saw it as an experiment of having the wearer be a bit like a puppeteer — wearing the object that is the shape of a human being. So that's how I see clothes. I don't care so much about fashion, actually. Kay does! I think I'm more interested in the poetics of fashion. That's why we tell stories.

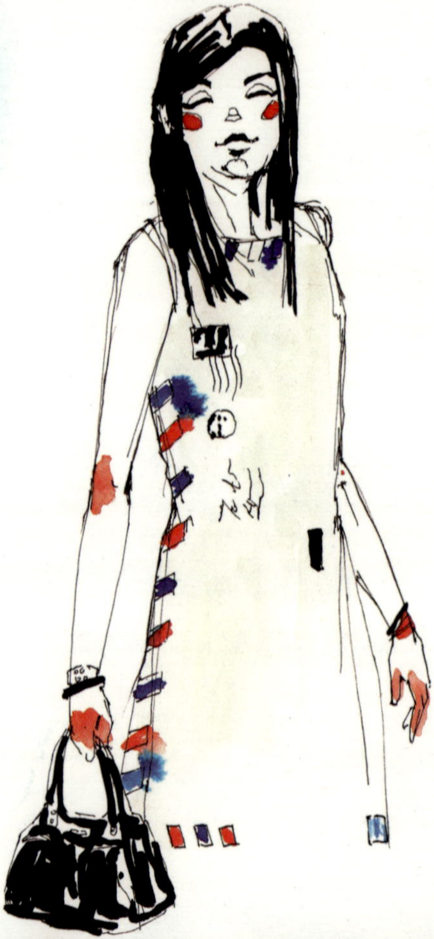

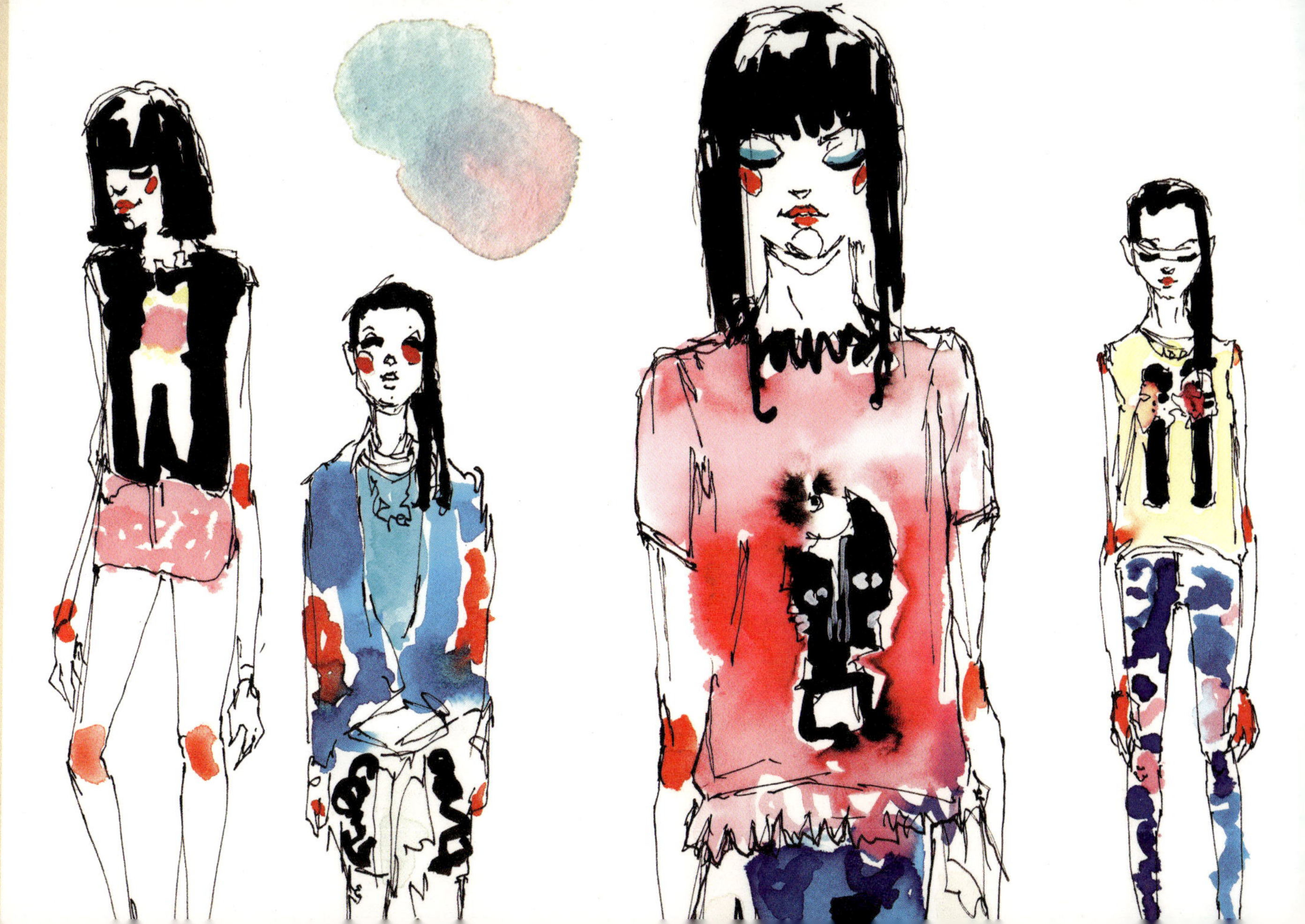

Tell us about the concept of storytelling through fashion.

Every season we have a story and the stories are very personally linked to us. The most intimate one was the letter one you saw, the air mail, because that was actually a letter to our dad, who passed away. It's like an attempt to communicate with him somehow, or to show him what we've done to make him proud.

We really admire how you and Kay just went for it, pursuing your dreams.

We feel it's not just a business. I think why we're so determined is because it feels like a mission. When we were young, people would look up to us in art because we got good grades. But Kay got really upset in the HKCEE [Hong Kong Certificate of Education Examination], the art course, she actually failed it.

Really?

Yes, you know the sketching? They expect you to sketch in pencil. But in the examination, she decided to use blue and watercolour and they failed her. She was always the one who was tipped to get an A in the class and she failed. It left a scar on her confidence. So that's one of the incidents that [led

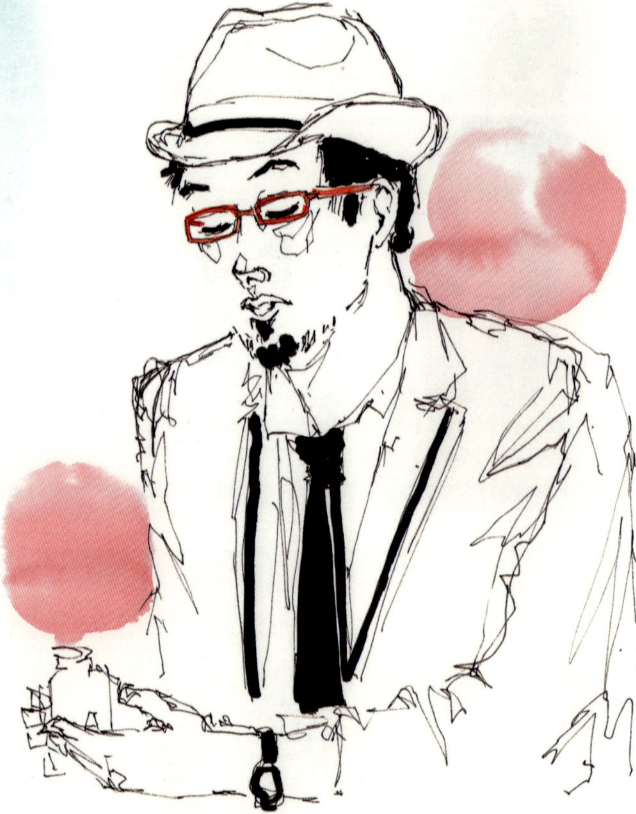

us to believe] we need to have this Daydream Nation where daydreamers and silly people or people who like to do weird things or slightly off-the-track things can feel that they're okay — it's not wrong or a bad thing to whistle down the street or tap dance while waiting for the bus or just dance when you're listening to music, or anything, just anything silly. I think that's why whatever happens, we have this strong urge to do something. Although I love Hong Kong, it's over-managed. It's too controlling. In London, there are so many street performances. In Hong Kong, I only ever see old people or beggars or blind people playing *erhu* and things like that. So when I first came back [in 2006], that was the first mission. I'd go to the streets every Sunday to busk. I did that for two years until I got too busy.

What do you love about Hong Kong?

Definitely living here is very. . . what's the word? Convenient and efficient. And how to describe it — my stomach is always very satisfied, even under a very limited budget! The good side of the city is all about being very efficient and quick and being at all places at the same time. You can buy stuff at Sham Shui Po then get maybe some art supplies in Mong Kok. All the places are so near and it's so handy. And at the same time, if you just want to leave it all behind, the city, the crowds, I can get to the beach in an hour. I can just take a ferry to Lantau Island. I think that's the interesting thing, it's so small but it's like a *mah jeuk* — a sparrow — it still has all the organs inside. Every-thing is compact, it's all there. That's what I like about Hong Kong.

What's your favourite way to spend a Sunday?

When I was still single, I spent my Sundays busking on the street. That went on for a while, even after I was in a relationship I still did that for many Sundays until she said, 'I have my ideal Sunday, too.' So from then on, we started spend-ing more time at the beach, going to places like Lantau Island or Cheung Chau.

Under the Bridge

I had seen her a million times before and never once had the courage to approach her. This time was different. I was here to learn, so why not just ask: *What exactly does she do?* I had a vague idea, but what little I knew of her practices, like some Chinese version of voodoo, had always frightened me a little.

What Mrs. Lum performs is a ritual known as *da siu yun* which literally translates to "hit the small person." With her little nest of incense and paper tigers, and a deity altar laid out on the sidewalk underneath a loud rumbling highway overpass, Mrs. Lum's vocation is to get rid of the "small people" in your life. Not in the Sopranos way, but with the gentler wish that their paths will not interfere with yours.

So I asked her how much she charges (HK$50) and whether she could show me what it is that she does (yes). She seemed as curious about me as I was about her. I was clearly a foreigner uneducated in the ways of her heritage. With a warm smile, she sat me down on a plastic stool. She asked my name, date of birth and who it was that I wanted to devote this "hitting the small person" ritual to. I drew a blank. I didn't have any enemies, not that I knew of at least. Never mind, she smiled. And softly, rhythmically she began

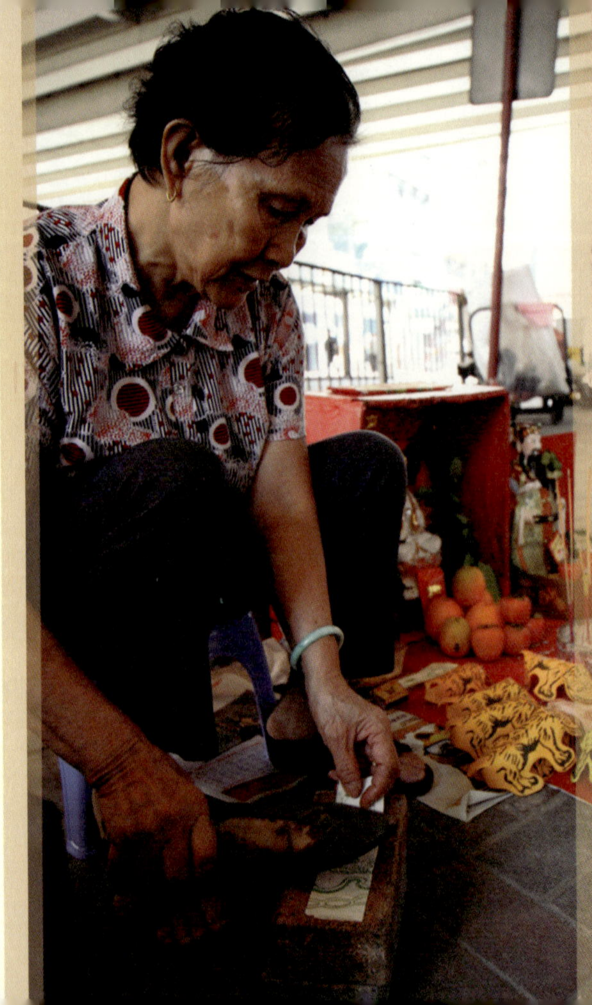

to chant with concentrated focus. She was totally absorbed, unaware of the thundering traffic, the non-stop river of people streaming past us, some of them curious and staring at what was happening. She lit a few incense sticks and threw rice on the paper tigers and on two pieces of raw chicken that I hadn't noticed until now. How strange, I thought. And then she took a piece of folded paper with green drawings of people on it, waved it in front of the incense and two burning candles, and placed it on top of a slab of brick. Chanting still, she took an old, grey, pointy-toed shoe (though the heel had been broken off) and began slapping the shoe against the piece of paper with surprising force. She then took a paper tiger, set it on fire and we watched it burn in a tin can. More paper still appeared, repeating the cycle of waving, lighting and watching it burn.

All the while, I found the chanting surprisingly serene and devotional, not nearly as scary or weird as I had anticipated. And when it was over, she took my hands, her kind eyes looking into mine, and told me everything was going to be alright. I believed her immediately, relaxed with the knowledge that I was blessed with good, protective spirits now; the bad ones were gone.

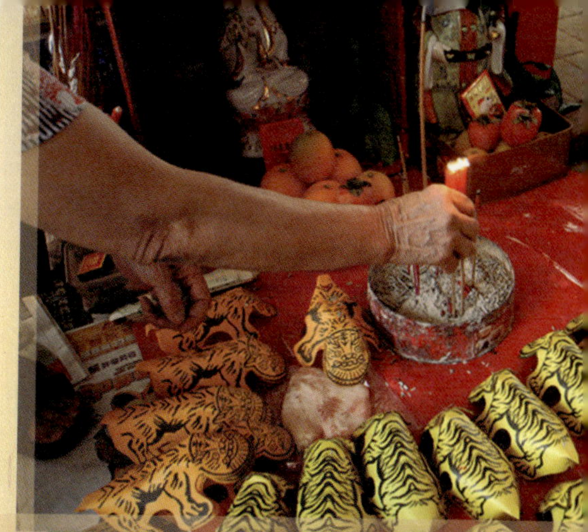

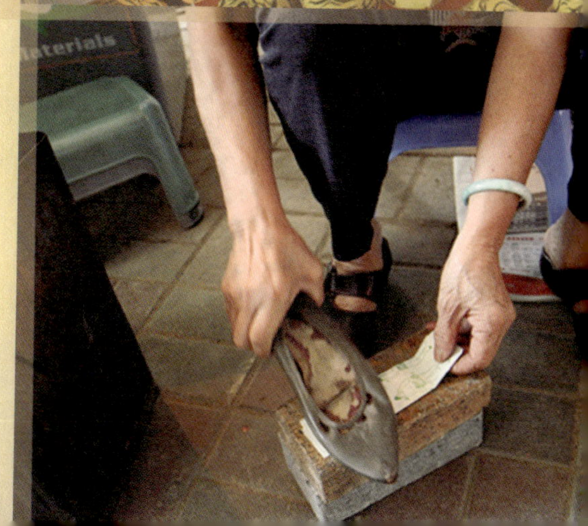

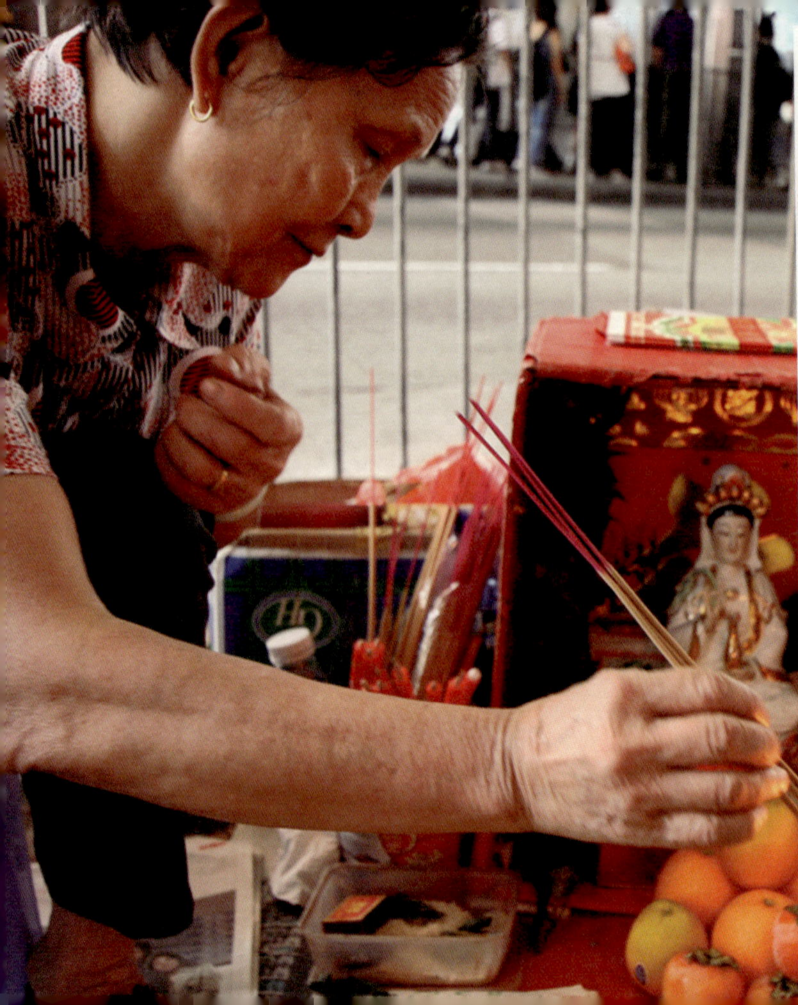

Q&A with Mrs. Lum

What is 'da siu yun'?
If your work isn't going well, you're not feeling well or your business isn't doing well, 'da siu yun' can help things go more smoothly. It brings a guardian spirit to assist you and the small people become distant.

How long have you been working here?
Many years.

How many hours do you work in a day?
From 8 or 9 a.m. to about 7 p.m.

How old are you?
I'm in my 70s.

How many children do you have?
Six children, more than 10 grandchildren.

Do you enjoy your work?
There's not much to do at home so I come out.

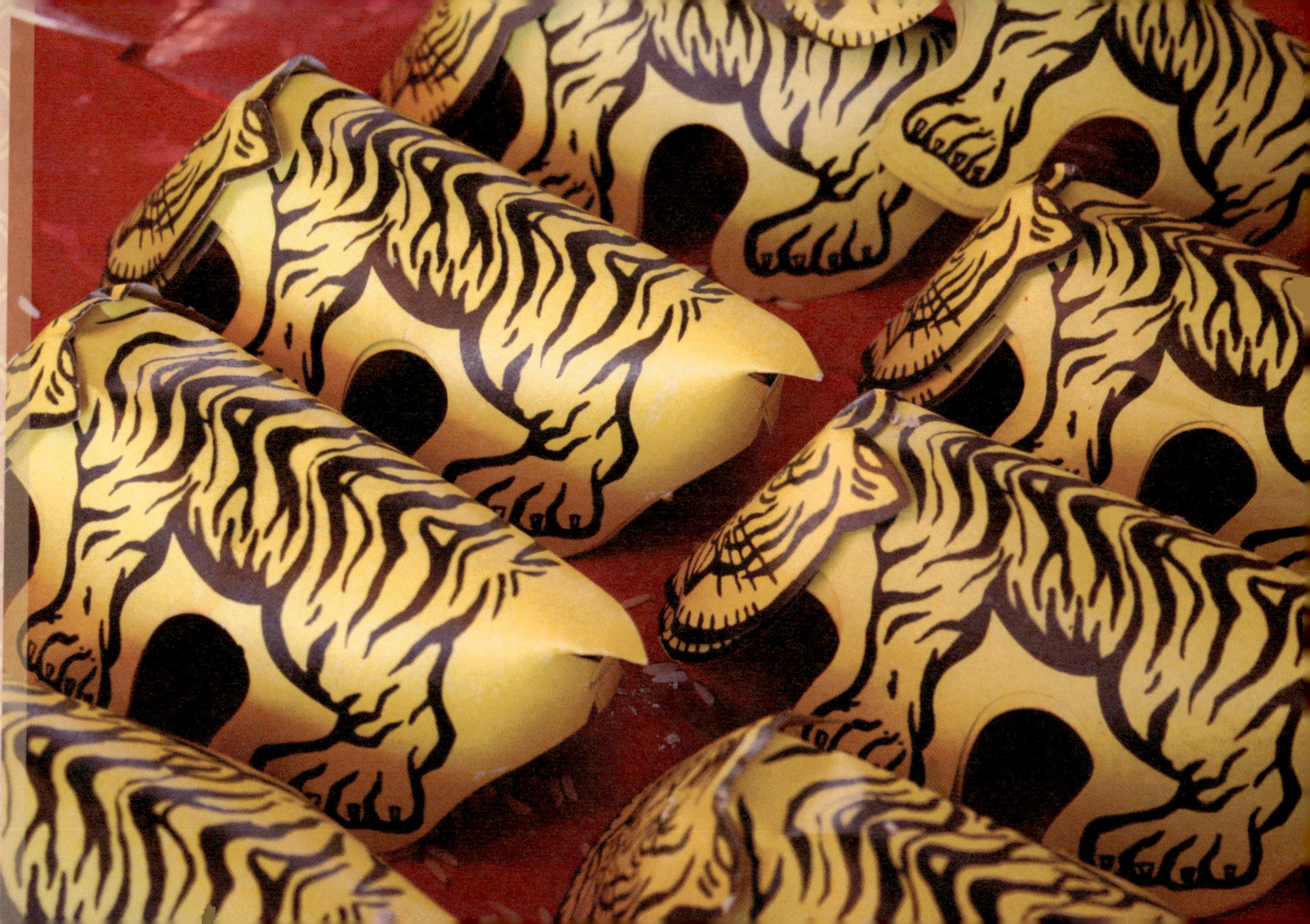

Find Magic in

STANLEY

A Perfect Evening When Nothing Much Happens

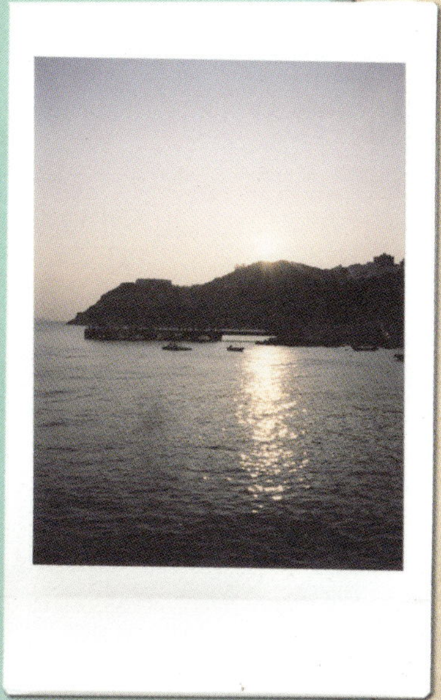

Stanley's one of those quintessentially touristy places that I just love. And while the discerning traveller isn't supposed to espouse the merits of a place *everyone knows about*, really, there's something to be said about the tried-and-true.

Stanley is made of summer: a languid air laces through its seaside promenade, weekenders hang out in bars facing the blue sea and tourists crowd through a quaint market selling local art – and knock-offs of more successful local art. But I probably feel particularly compelled to write about Stanley because I came here several years ago on a magical evening with great friends. It was one of those perfect holiday nights, with perfect weather, perfect food, mesmerizing music and just enough discovery to make it all feel special.

The day had already started off pretty darn great. Howard, a friend and truly one of the best hosts in the world, had taken the day off to take me and Nick, my brother, and a couple of our friends to Ocean Park. Howard's perennial enthusiasm never wanes with age, and if there's someone who could inspire us to run wild around a theme park like giddy children, it'd be him. We spent the day cooing at baby pandas, marvelling at jellyfish and riding daredevil rides (well, okay, I watched while they did) and by the end of the afternoon, I was feeling happy, sweaty and replete.

Normally this is where I'd call it a day. But Howard's all about *carpe diem*, seize the day. So with that, he asked: "Where to next? Stanley or Shek O?" After short deliberation, we settled on dinner at Stanley.

It was dusk by the time we arrived, the sky melting into light purples and deep blues. It was quiet with the market closed and the tourists long gone. We took a walk down to the waterfront and watched the empty boats bobbing in the water. Dinner was delicious at the beautiful Murray House and afterwards, we took a long walk in the dark along the promenade that gave way to a narrow, concrete pathway that led to who-knows-where. We went up some steps, then down some more, discovered a temple along the way and walked along a deserted sidewalk that led us to a supermarket housed in a heritage building where we bought red bean popsicles before continuing our evening stroll. There was nothing particularly momentous about that night. But when I think of that evening, I'm instantly brought back to the warmth of the air, the current of laughter, the ease that flowed and the happiness of being far away with some of my favourite people in the world.

That night has stayed with me long after it was over, reminding me that travel is so often more about what we feel than what we do. And whether we choose to see this world solo or with friends and family, to journey far and wide or stay close to home, magic can be found in the quietest of corners when there seems to be nothing to do and nothing to see.

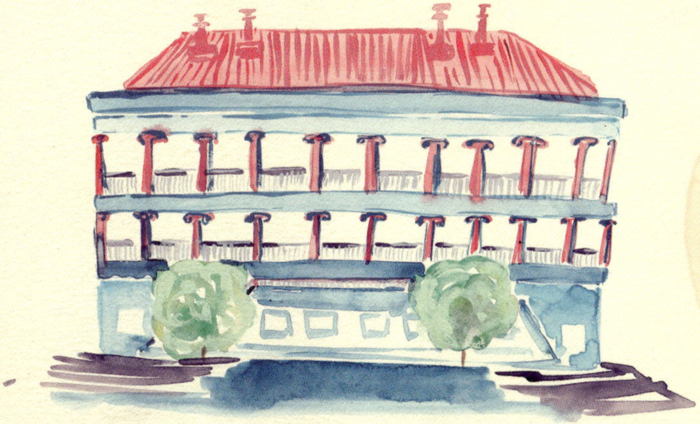

Two Years Later. . .

After an unexpectedly stressful morning, Nick and I needed a break. We had come to Hong Kong for a creative adventure, to be moved by the city's rhythms, to amble its sidewalks and find inspiration in the people. But even here, on our blissful vacation halfway across the world from our normal reality, we found the heavy topics of money and jobs careening through our minds. So, if we were to be weighed down by such substantial subjects, we decided to do so in style. Standing at the bus depot on the south side of the island, we wondered where to go next. Then the rumble of a double-decker came to a stop before us with a sign that read "Stanley."

Of course! That was exactly where we needed to go. We hopped on the bus and found ourselves a short while later sitting on the most beautiful verandah in all of Hong Kong.

Well, "most beautiful" might be a point of debate. There are other colonial buildings in Hong Kong featuring perfectly lovely balconies. But this one in Murray House is our favourite with its checkerboard floors, whirring fans and hefty, pockmarked columns that frame the shimmering sea beyond.

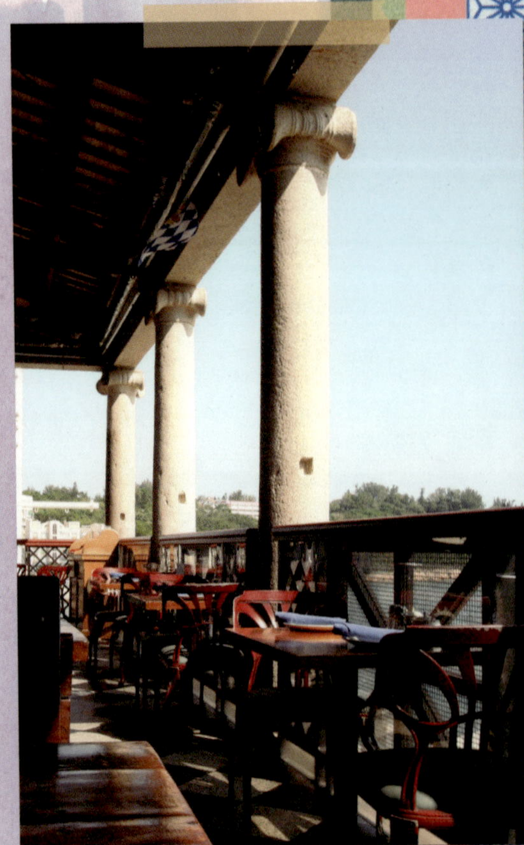

Murray House was constructed in 1846, five years after Hong Kong was ceded to British rule. It was originally located in the heart of Central until development gave way to the prism-like Bank of China tower. In 1982, the former military building was dismantled into 4,000 pieces, each one of them meticulously numbered and stored. It would take almost a decade before the government proposed its reconstruction in Stanley, where it now stands, home to several lovely restaurants.

Dining at Murray House is always a romantic affair, though you need not be with a lover to enjoy it. Our first meal here was on that languid evening in the fall of 2007 with Howard and friends. We spent the evening at Mijas, a Spanish tapas restaurant, dining on salted fish and Spanish meatballs and listening to a Filipino trio strum The Beatles' "Friends and Lovers" (our request). In the pitch black of the night, we couldn't see the horizon, but felt the lapping of waves nonetheless.

This morning was bright, blazing and hot — a million miles away from that night, but the magic of Murray House was no less. We felt lighter from the moment we arrived. And by the time we were seated and facing the blue sea with glasses of Riesling in hand, life seemed to have naturally unknotted itself a little.

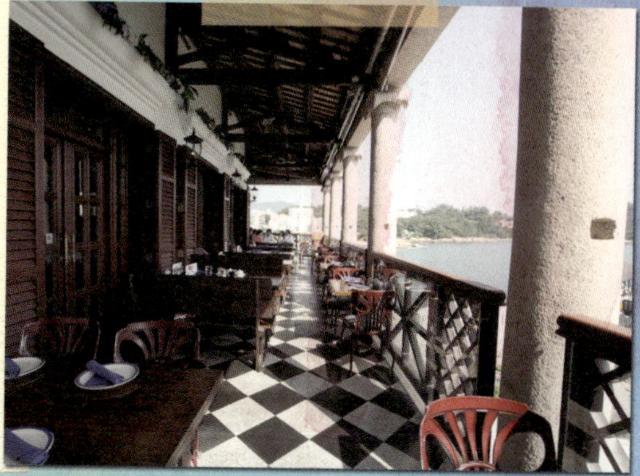

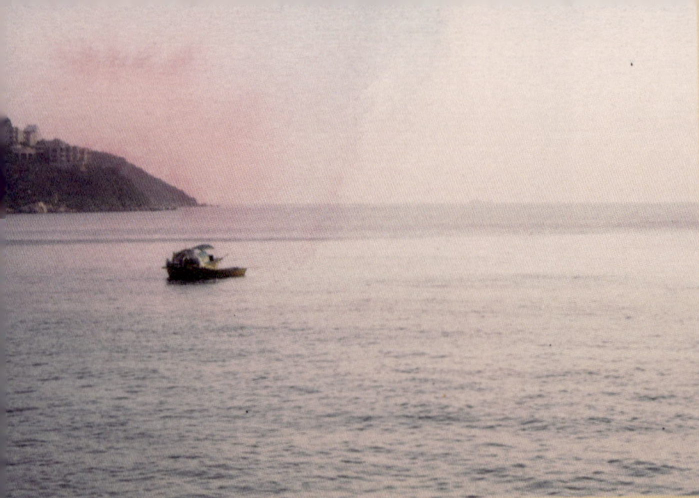
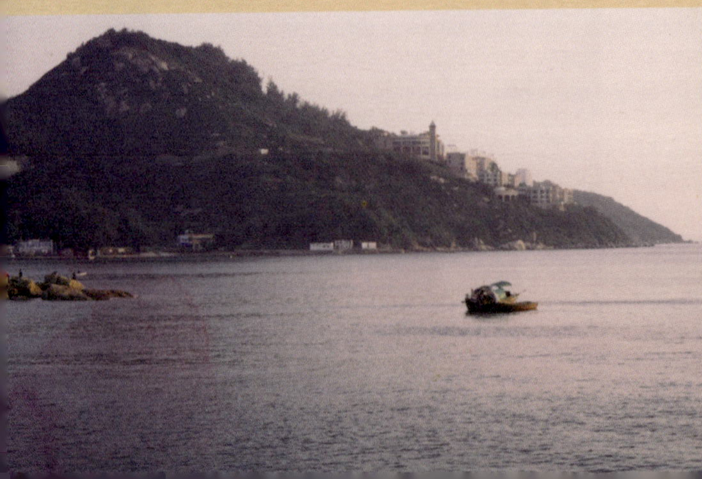
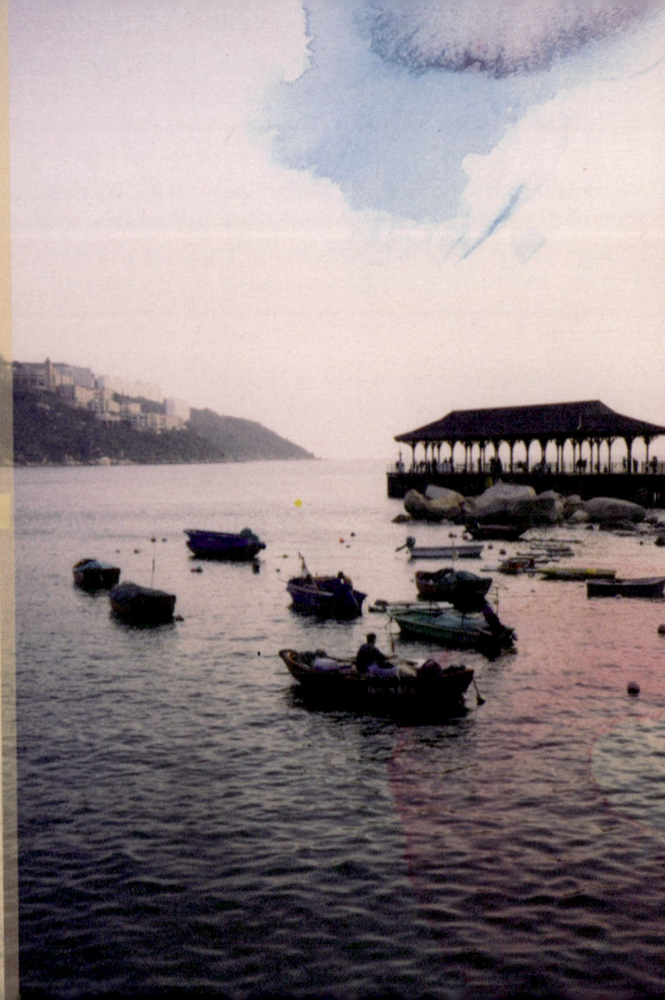

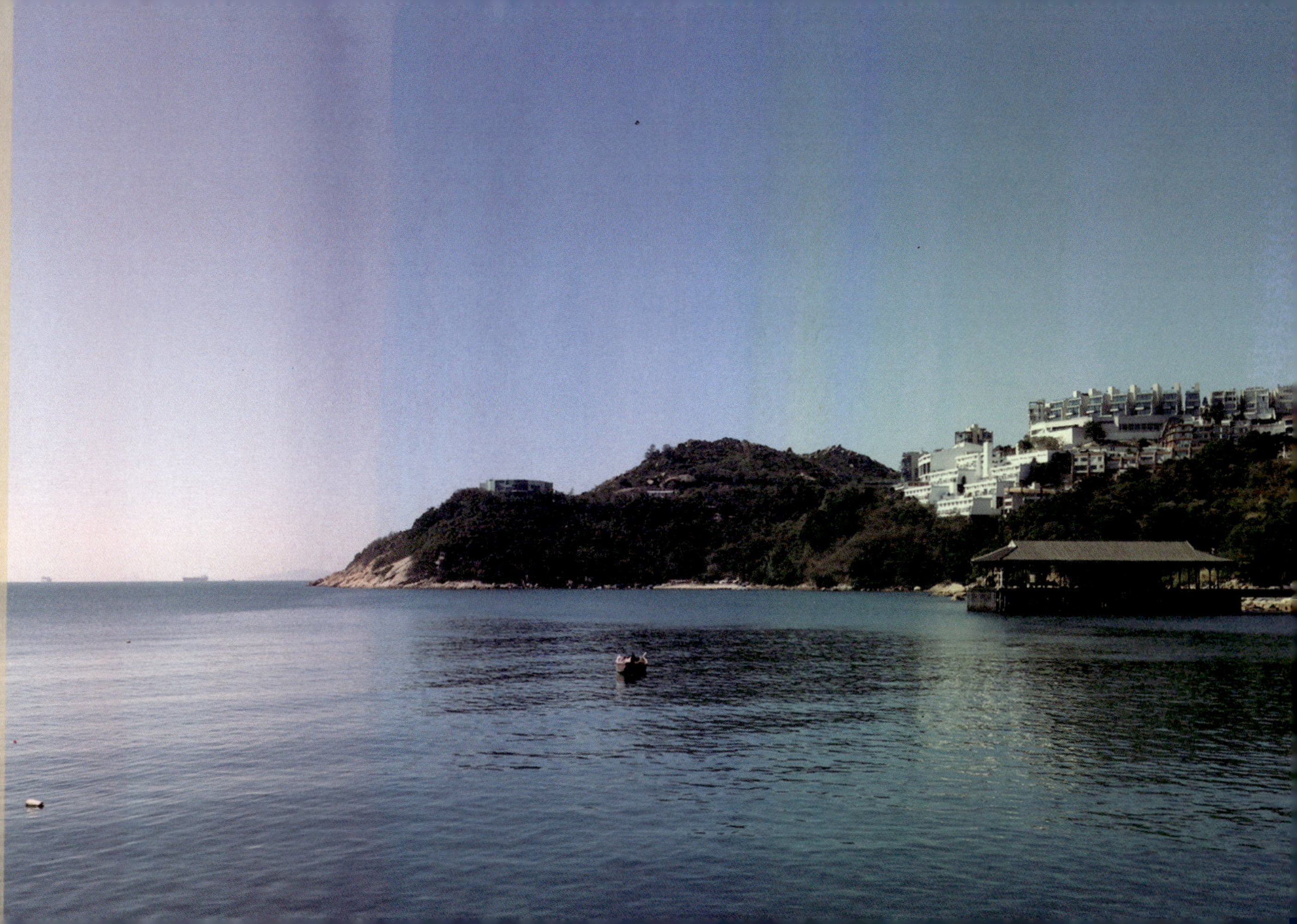

Step Back in Time in

Tai O

Welcome to Tai O

The bus wound its way uphill, chugging slowly like a roller-coaster car before the descent. I was slightly nervous. With the advancements of modern transportation, getting to this emerald island no longer requires the hour-long boat ride it once did — hop on the MTR and half an hour later you're there. But once on Lantau Island, I had not accounted for the long and twisty journey to the northwest of the island, where our destination of the day awaited.

We were headed to Tai O, a small, 300-year-old fishing village where people still live in wooden-stilted houses that rest above cloudy jade water. I'd seen photos of this village — beautifully romantic photos — but never visited until now.

Our bus was crammed full of Hong Kongers sitting shoulder to shoulder on this hazy Saturday afternoon. In front of us were two older men with their fishing rods. Next to us a large family of aunts and uncles, children and cousins, each one carrying multiple plastic bags bulging with meat, bread, napkins, paper plates and all manner of barbeque paraphernalia. No one else seemed to be nervous; but I am not very brave and as we climbed higher and higher, past verdant hillside and squat palm trees, I could feel my heart do a tiny flip-flop. A circular red sign indicated with alarm: Very steep hill. I took a deep breath... here we go.

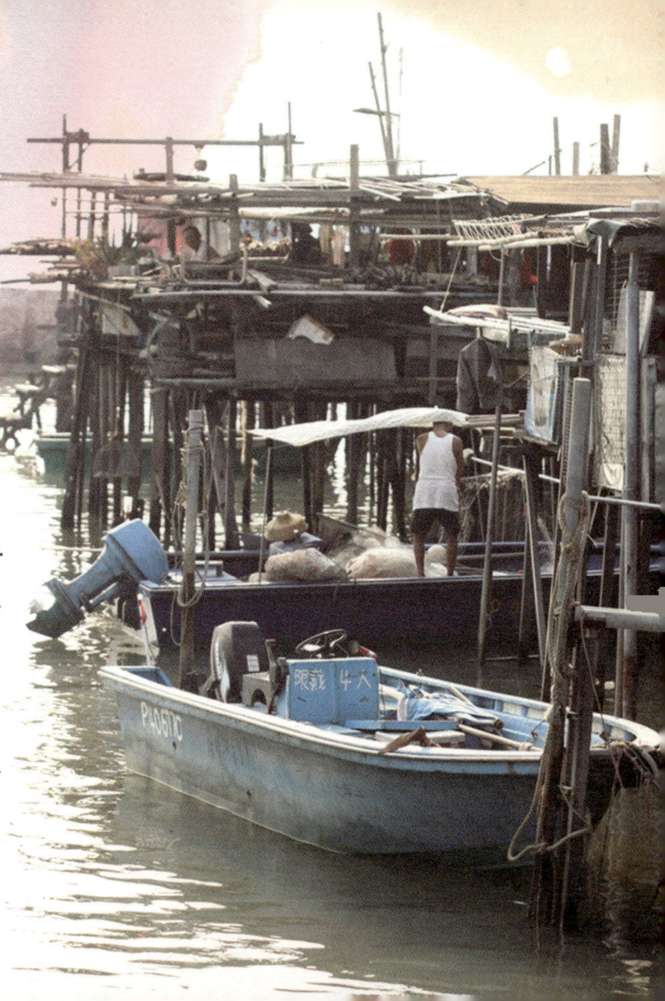

Our driver manoeuvred deftly downhill, hugging the lush hillside as open, blue water revealed itself far below. I wasn't sure whether to be stunned by this beauty, or alarmed at our great speed. The hair-raising turns and steep descent eventually gave way to gentler ground and before we knew it, we were bumping along at sea level. Brown cows grazed by the roadside (and sometimes into traffic); waves crashed into the long, narrow beach that followed the island's voluptuous curves. We passed a prison with million-dollar views, which seems incongruous and, at the same time, perfectly logical. Could being here, surrounded by the zen of the ocean, bring inner peace to even the most hardened criminals? I'd like to think so.

As our bus trundled along, past a muddy river with jumping fish, I thought it was a sure sign we were near. We disembarked at the last stop to a somewhat disappointing scene. Sure, there were boats moored at the pier, but no signs of the romantic, floating houses we had come to see.

We followed the crowd down a lane lined with market stalls on either side. Curled up, waxy balls of *fa gau* (dried fish air bladders apparently good for the skin) hung translucent in the late afternoon sun; the salty air mixed with a pungent, fishy scent. Charming, but not what we had expected – until we turned the corner and were met with a wide ribbon of water, a metal bridge and silvery light cast upon the

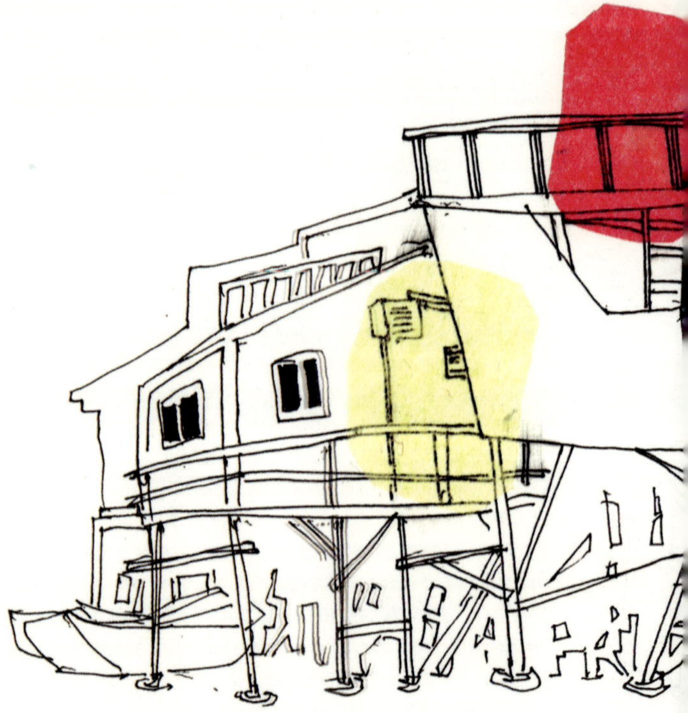

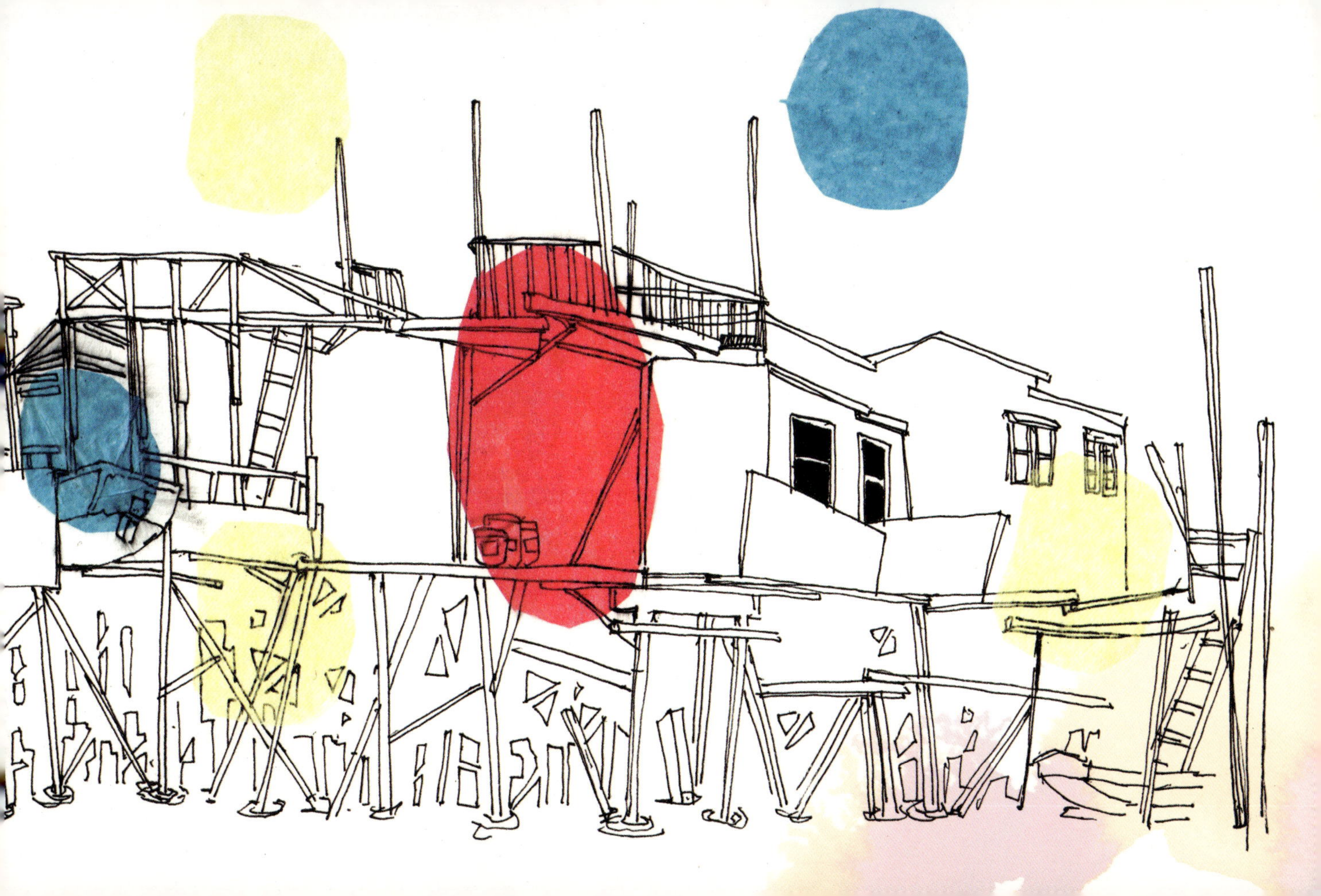

rooftops of houses with skinny legs. It was like walking into a traveller's dream. Except this wasn't some off-the-grid, undiscovered gem. This was Hong Kong and we were surrounded by tourists and photographers everywhere. Still, we found ourselves lost in the village's warren of shops and ramshackle homes. A fisherman glided gently by in his boat. Bright red chili peppers lay baking in the sun. Fish were hung to dry next to someone's laundry.

We finally found it. Welcome to Tai O.

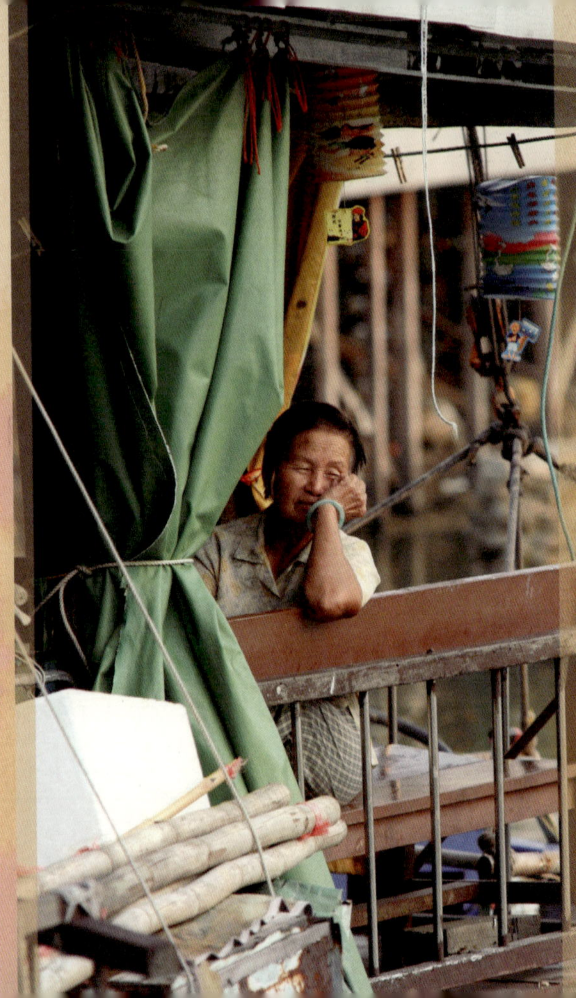

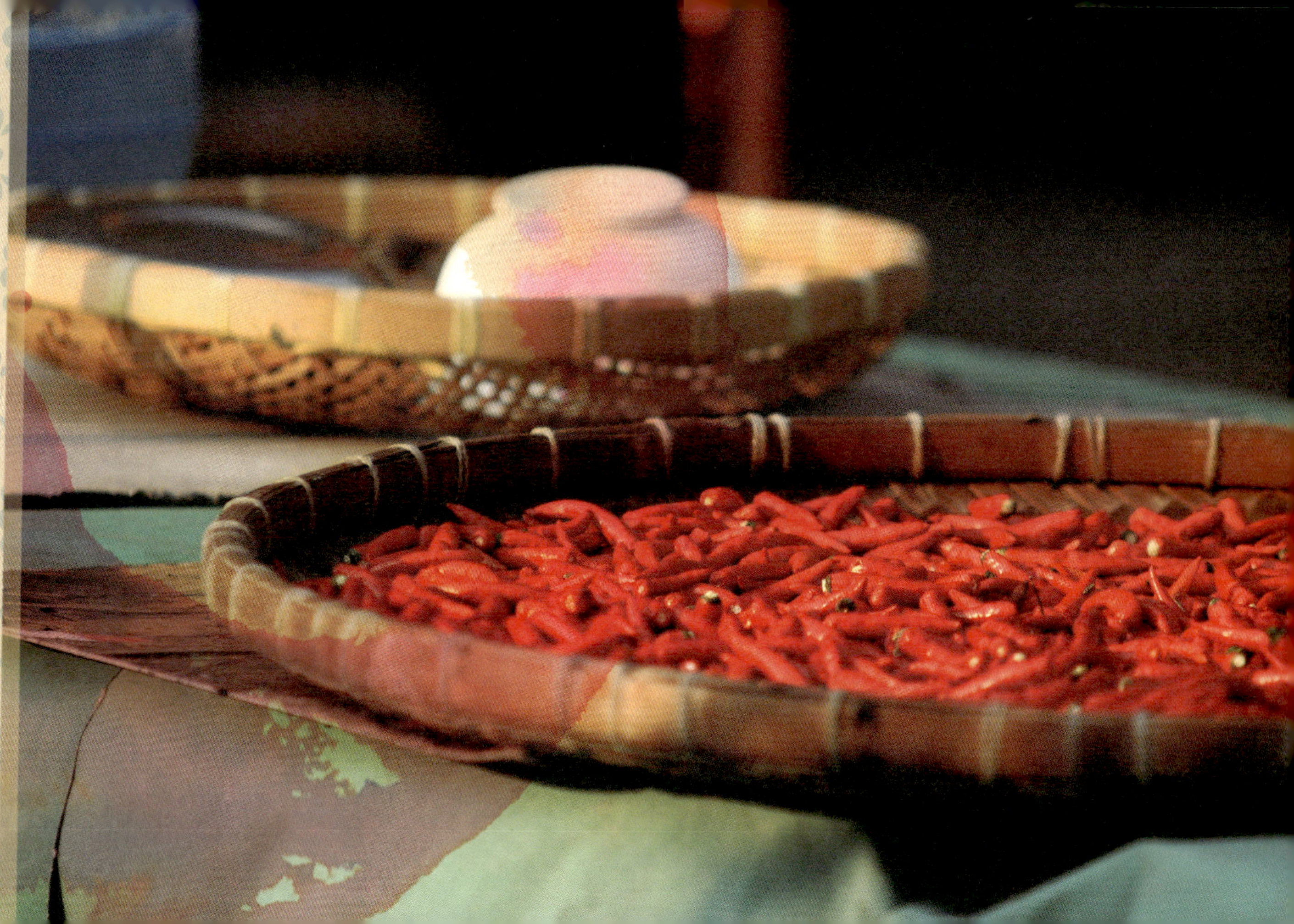

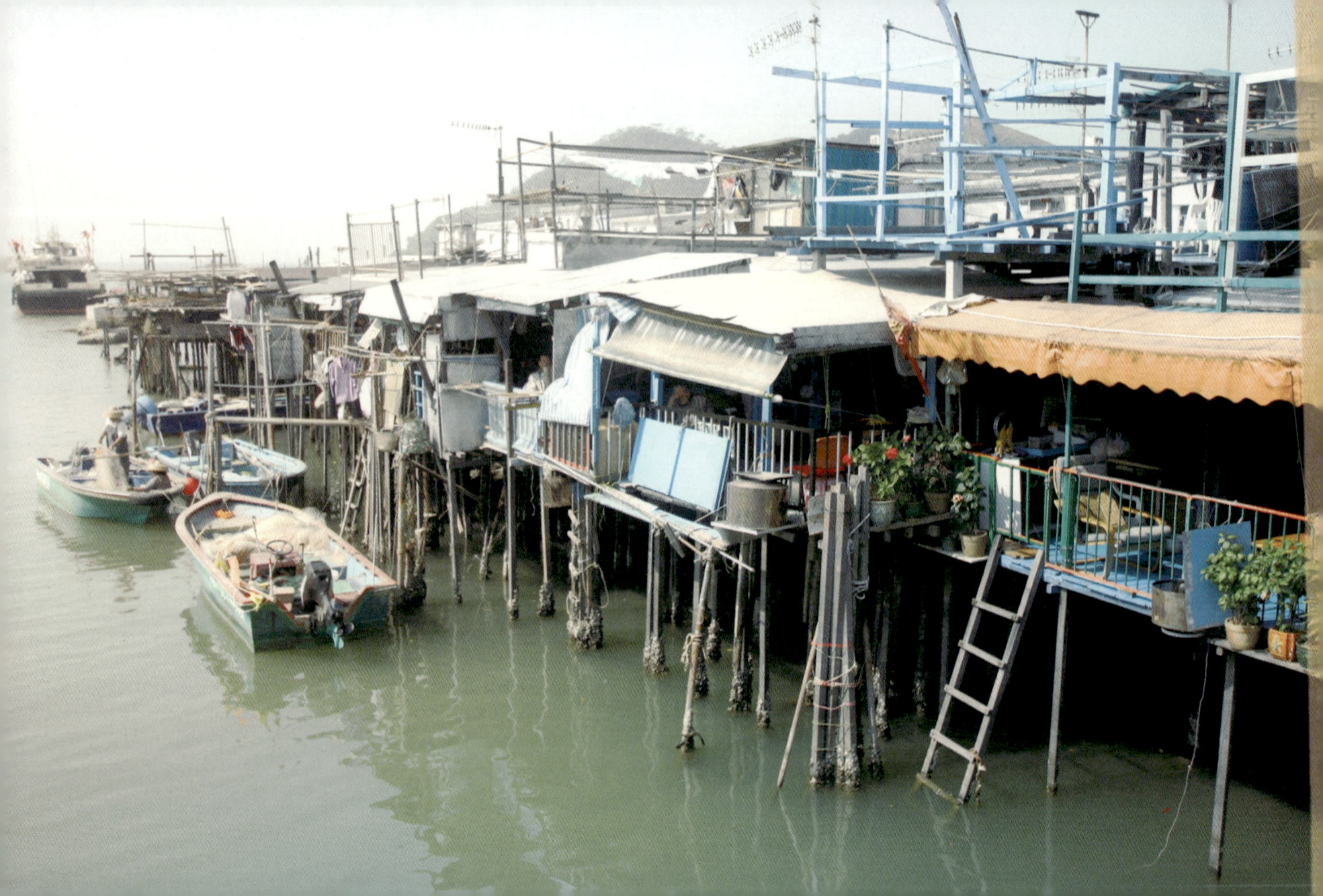

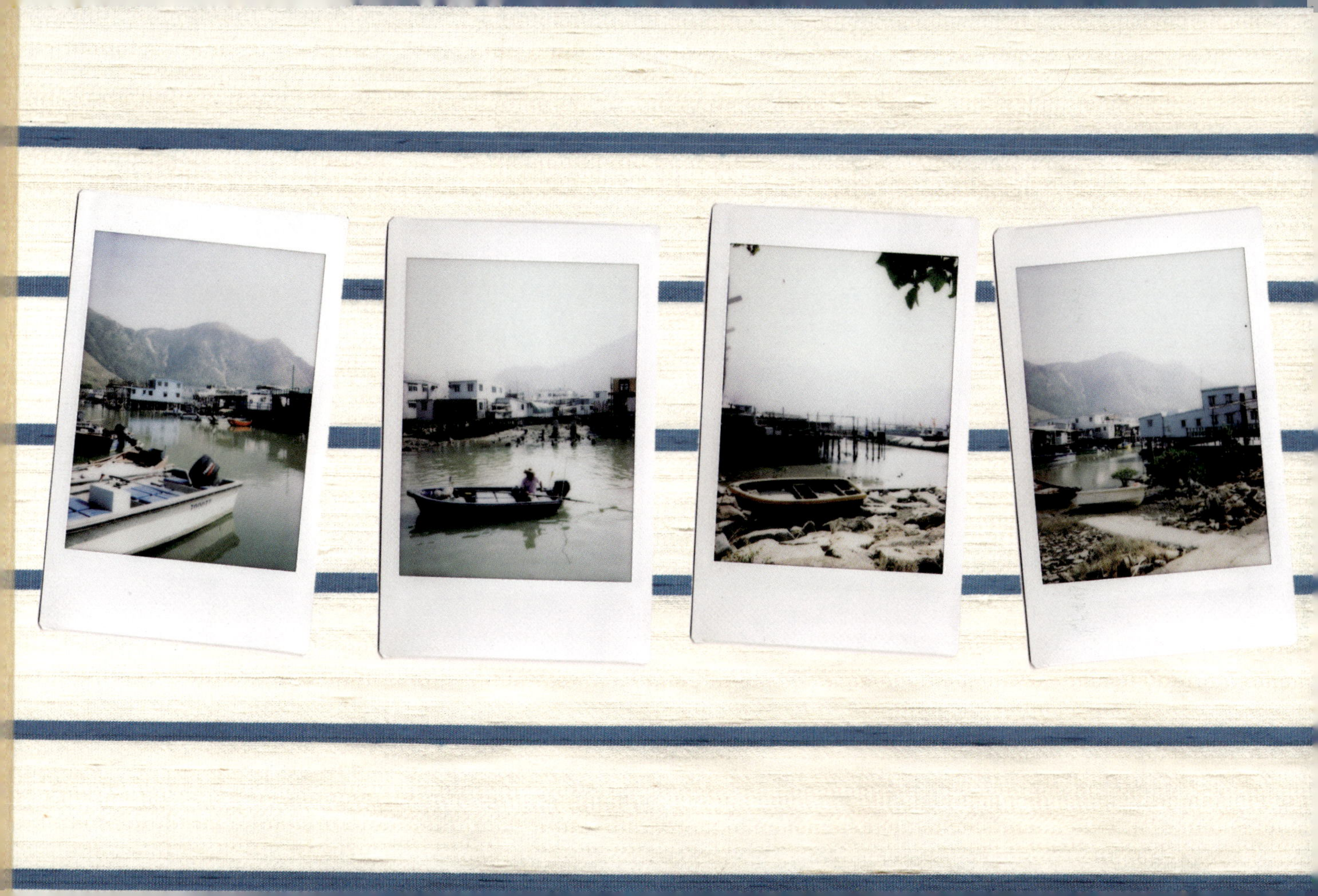

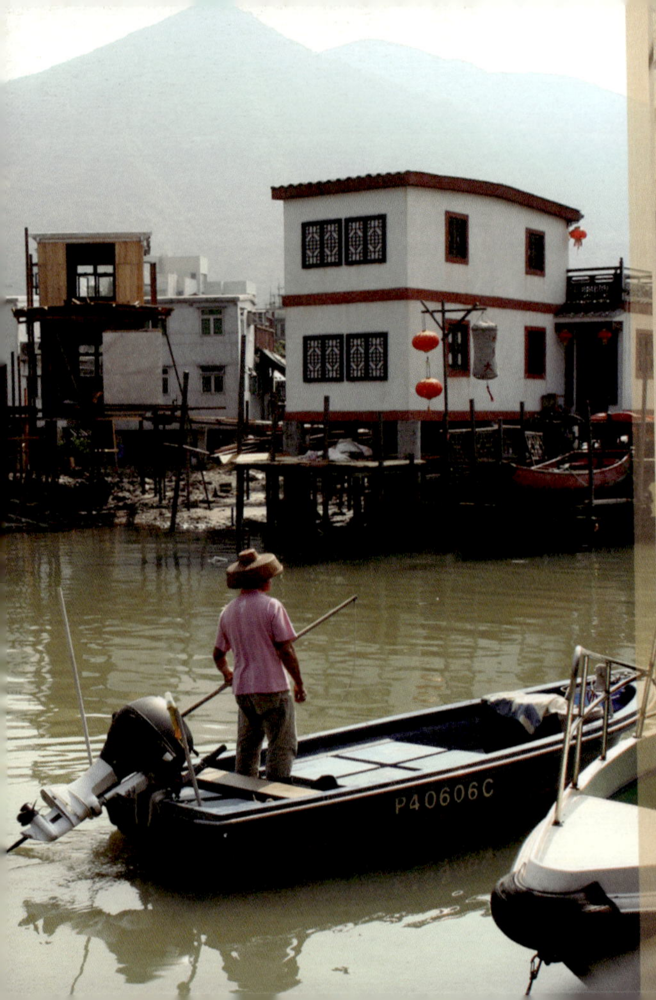
P40606C

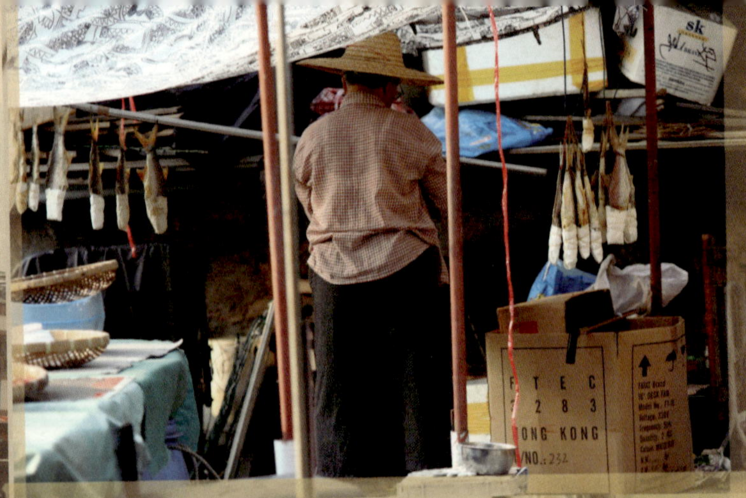

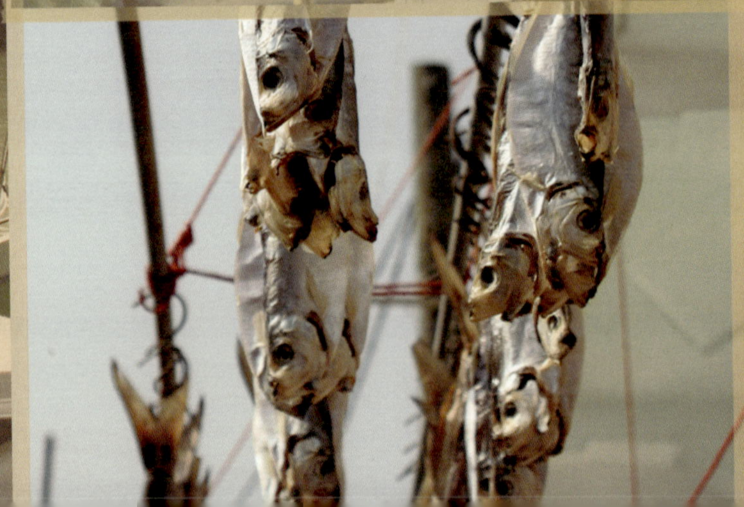

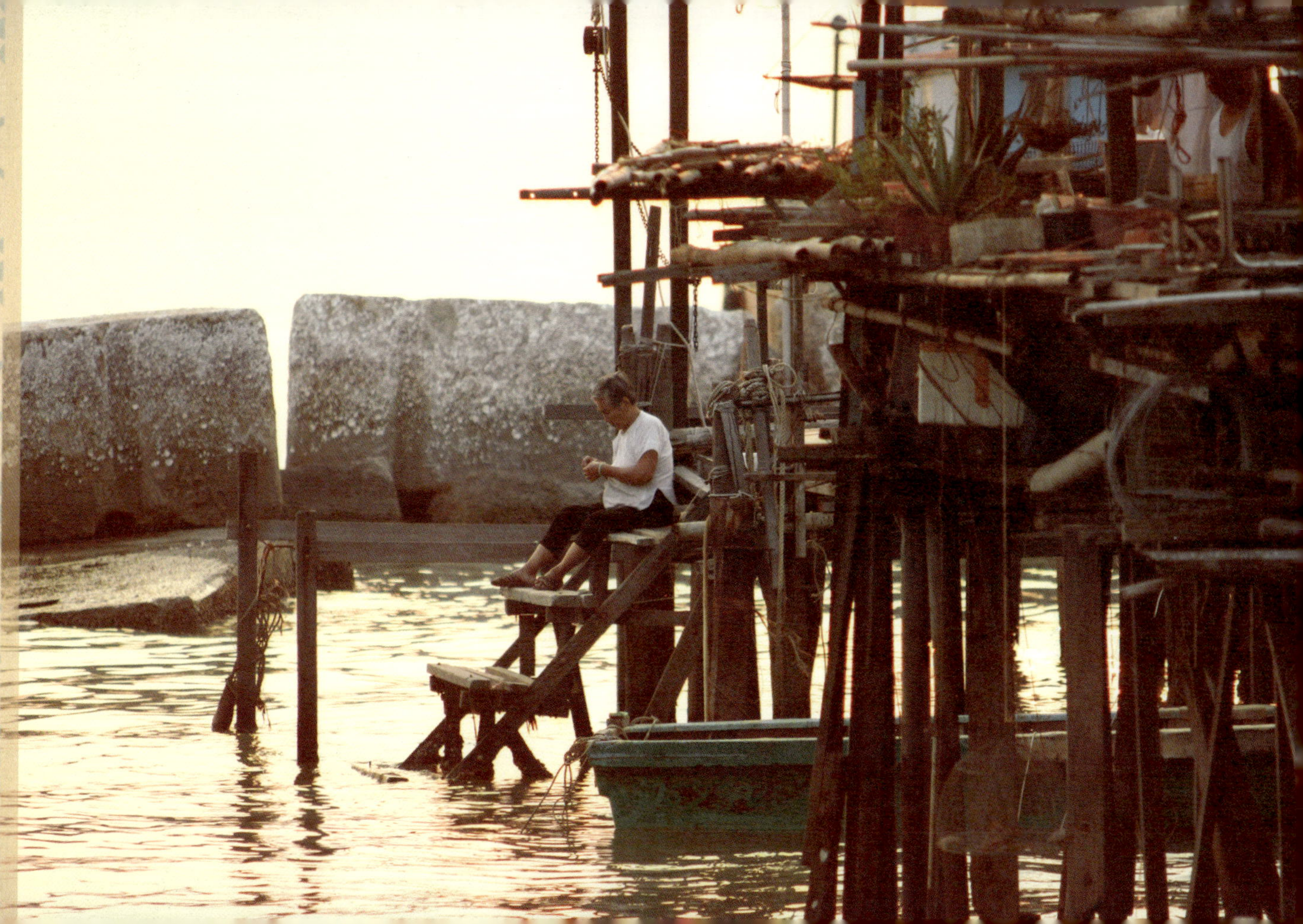

Be a Local in NORTH POINT

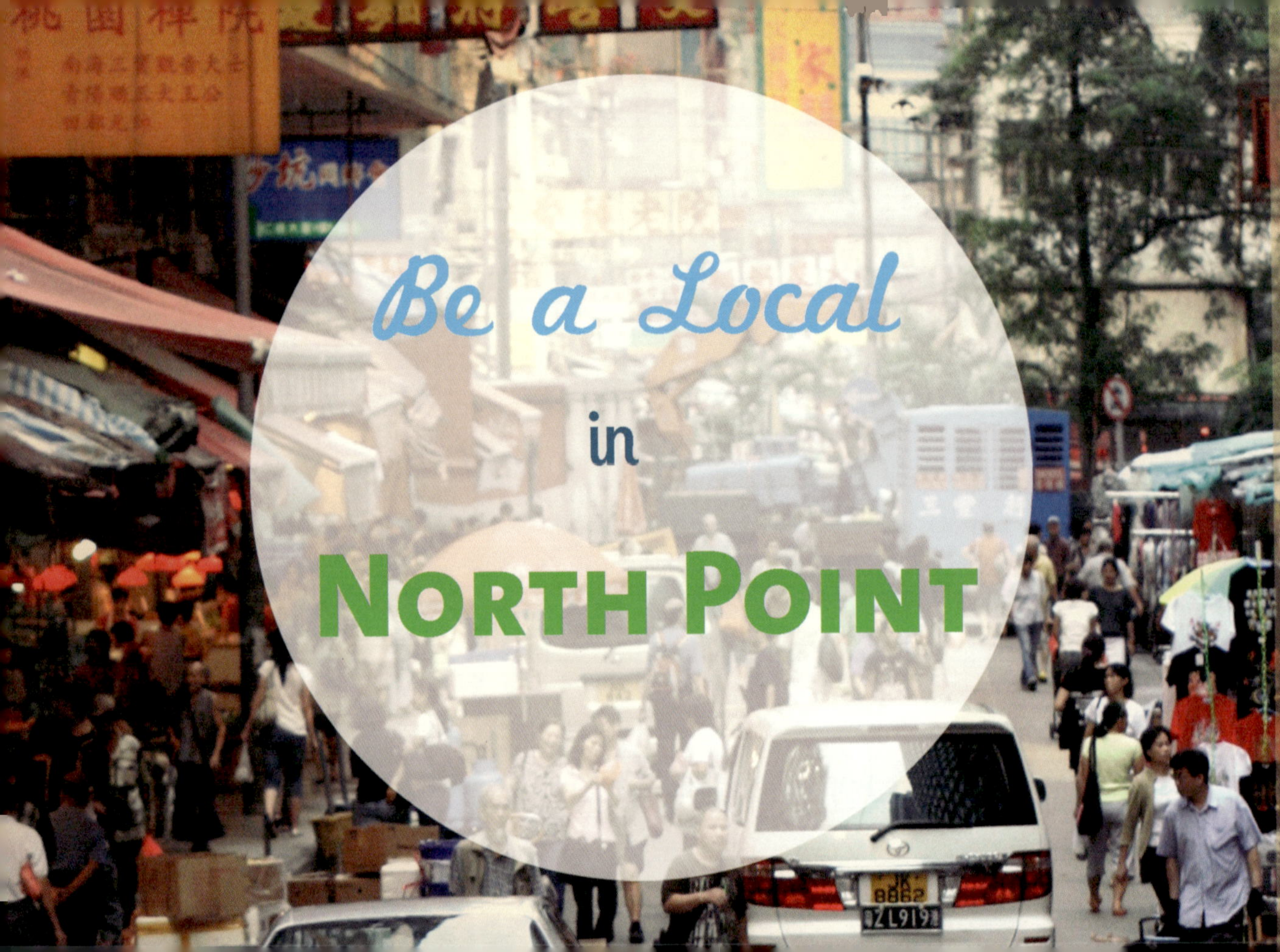

North Star

Some people look to the north star to take them home; we look for North Point. Staggering off the bus after a long flight to the warm air, a quiet morning and my parents waiting with big smiles, I always know when we've arrived.

It's almost always early morning when we reach North Point and the first thing that hits us is the intense smell of gasoline from boats in the harbour, a hazy blue sky and the rare sight of a half-empty pier. We roll our suitcases towards my parents' flat, past King's Road where the sky disappears behind massive residential blocks dusted grey with time, looking worn and disorderly with air conditioners jutting out and washing hanging out from the windows. That's the thing about North Point: It's not very pretty. I'd say it's unremarkable at best with no significant monuments to speak of or cool boutiques to show. Yet when friends visit, this is where I want to take them.

The markets, the bakery across the street with egg tarts to die for, the din of Cantonese and the friendly Chinese medicine doctor waving from her shop window are just a few of the things that make us feel at home. For us, travel has always been about slowing down and experiencing life through another lens. Here, we slip right in to an easy rhythm and the pleasures of daily life.

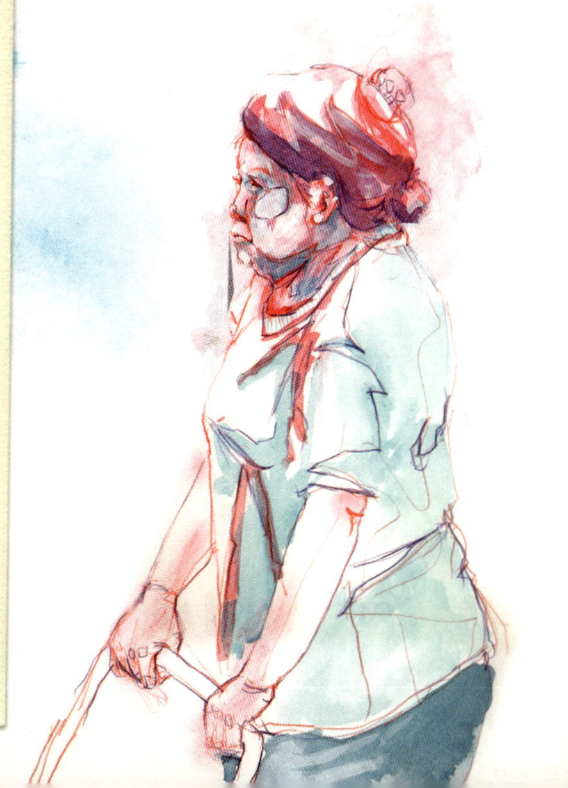

Wet Markets

Growing up, the wet markets of Hong Kong held a great fear for me. They harboured feathered demons with razor beaks, beady soulless eyes and red fleshy skin flapping on top of malicious visages.

Yes, you know the evil of which I speak: chickens.

Some people think I'm exaggerating but the fear was, and remains, real and debilitating. I have no idea where or how this fear was developed; I only know I've always lived in fear of these feathered fowl. Which is a shame considering how they seem to proliferate in places I tend to enjoy travelling most, such as the rice fields of Bali, rural villages of Africa and, of course, the markets of Hong Kong.

Wet markets have been around for well over a century in the city, with the oldest one in Central more than 140 years old (though sadly, Graham Street Market may not be around for much longer as it's earmarked for redevelopment). Long a daily ritual for locals, my mother is prone to losing herself in them, even though she has a helper to do all the shopping. Dashing off "for a few minutes," it's not unusual for her to return two hours later with triumphant stories of seam-stresses doing good as they save every hard-earned $10 bill

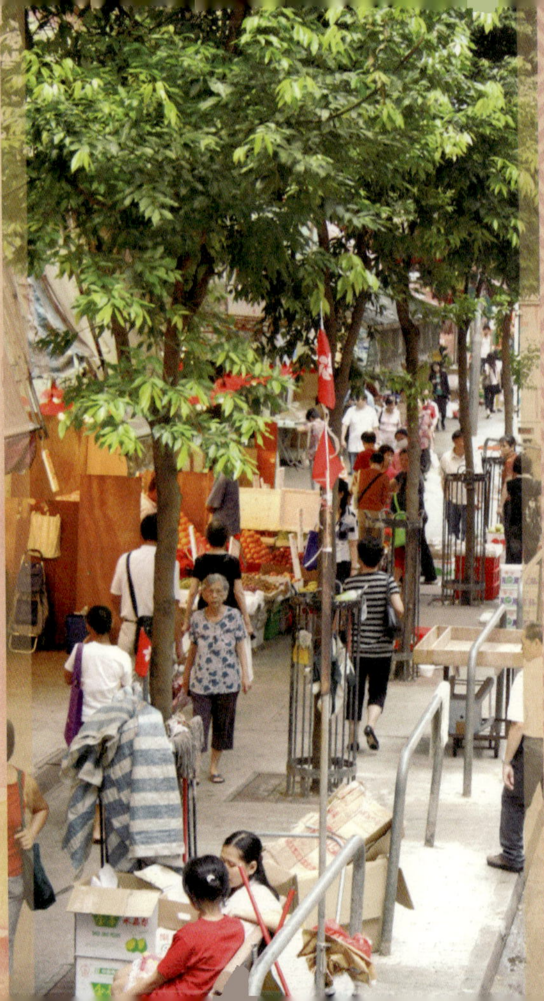

to send their kids to university, or finding a special, hand-beaded slipper that reminds her of her childhood. But of course it's really all about the freshest food one can get, and what could be fresher than a just-slaughtered chicken?

Perhaps the one good thing to come out of avian flu, then, is that the sale of live chickens is declining in popularity. The government has for years been offering cash incentives to live poultry sellers to give up their licences. It's working — the number of vendors declined to about 130 in 2012 from 800 in 2004. Which allows me to finally enjoy the clanging chaos of an outdoor wet market, taking in the bellowing traders yelling "*ah jei!*" to passing shoppers, aproned produce sellers carefully arranging fruit in pyramidical fashion and weighing a catty of *gai lan* under iconic red lamps. With fresh fish flipping on beds of ice and the chop of cleavers on wooden blocks, this is the kind of mess that Hong Kong excels at. I love this part of the city, with its colour and smells and crowds swirling into a happy sort of pandemonium. It feels, finally, just like home.

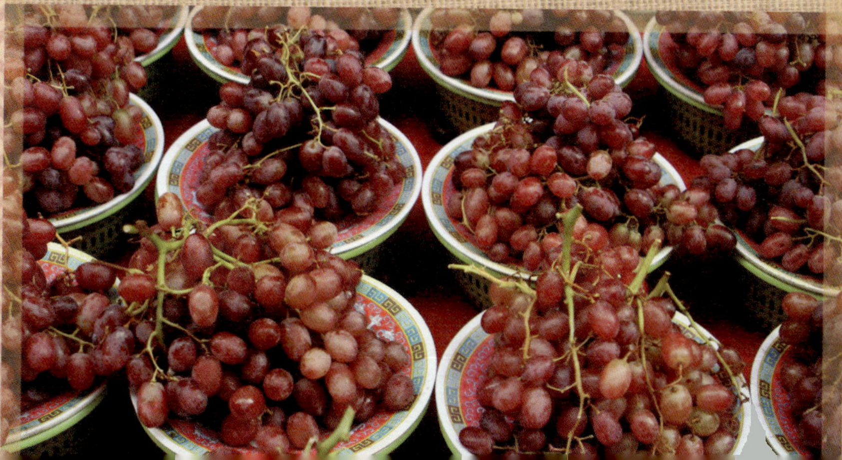

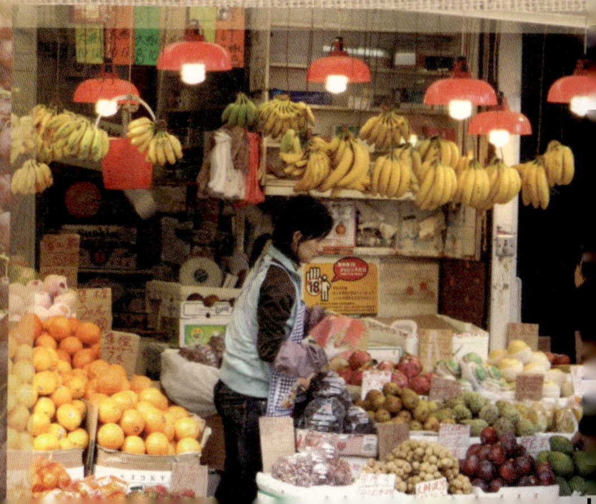

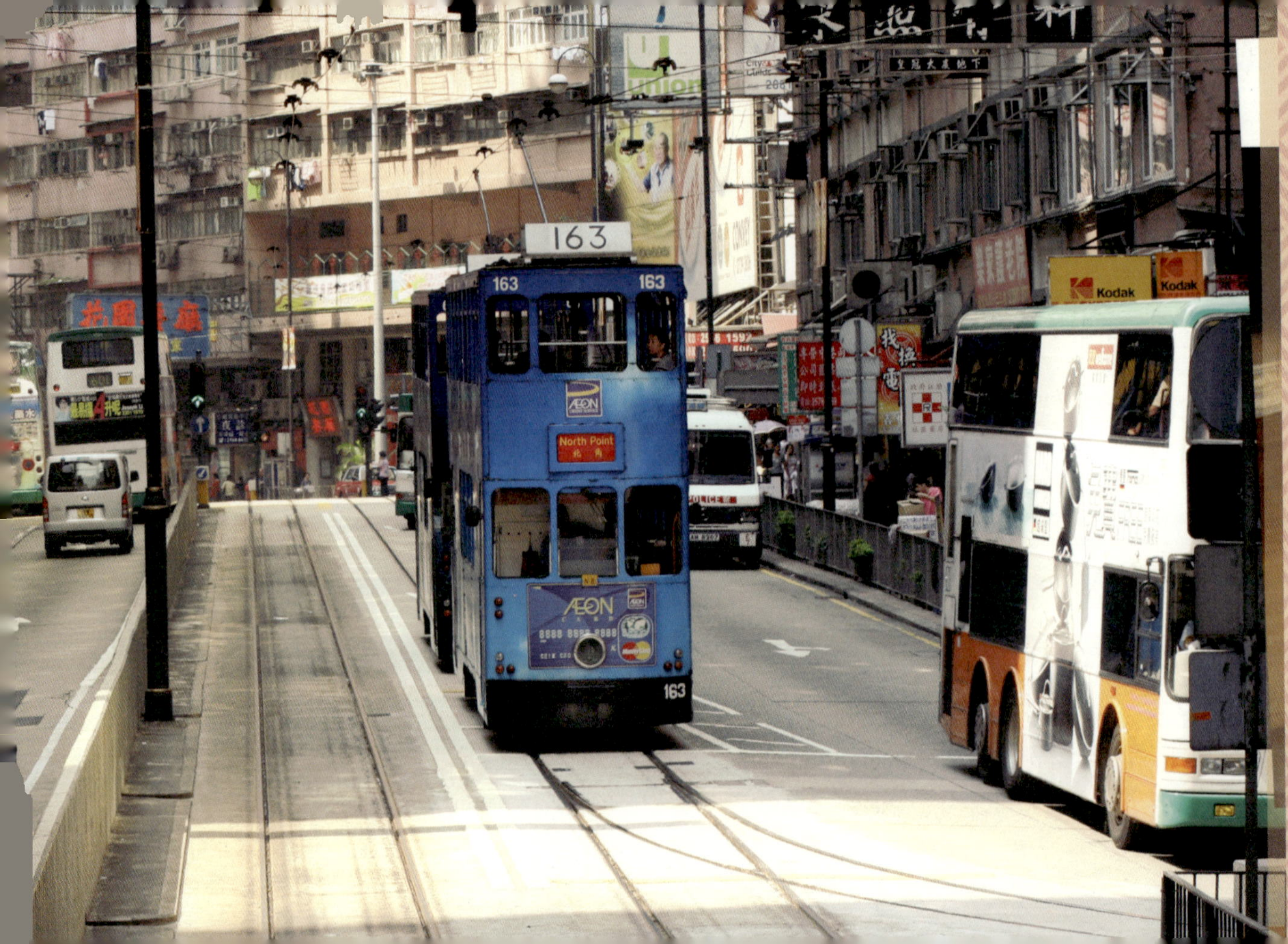
163
163
163
North Point
北角
AEON
163
Kodak
Kodak

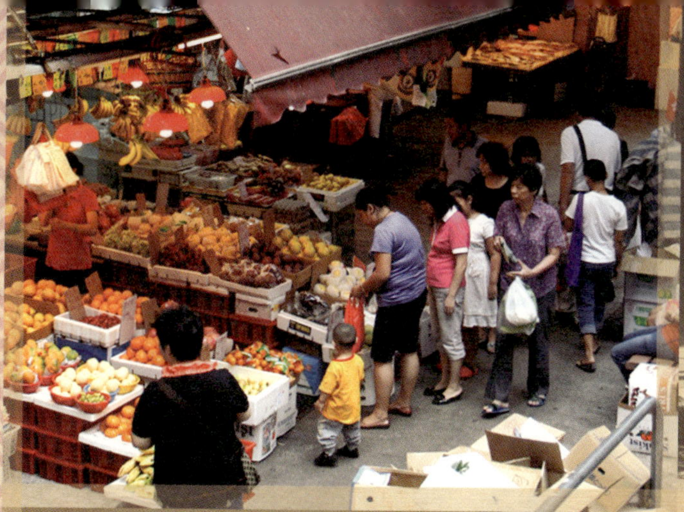
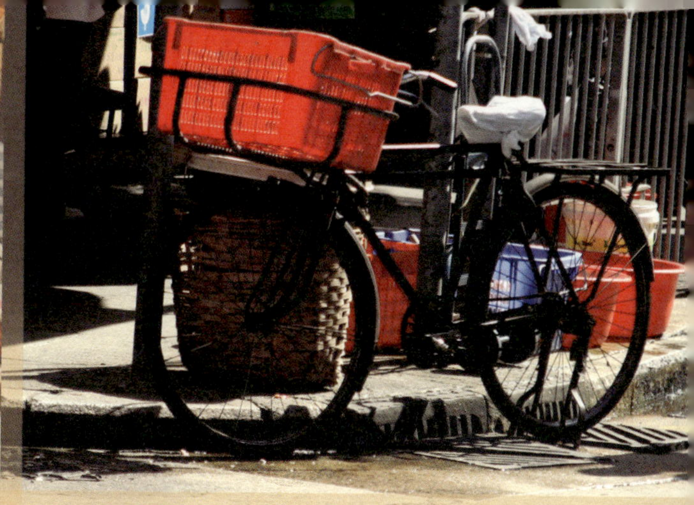
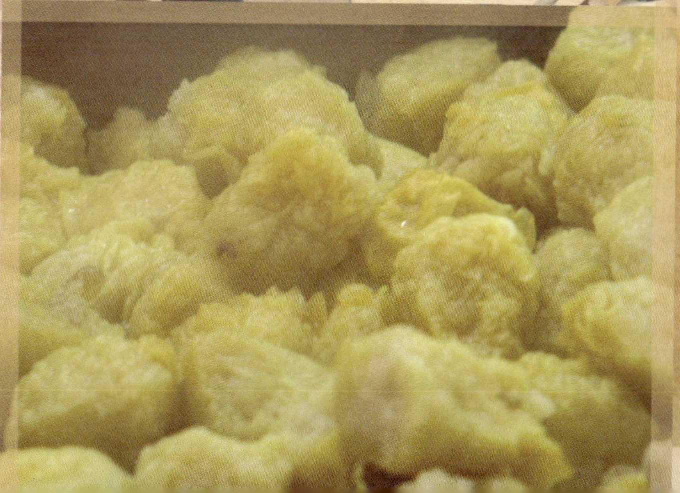
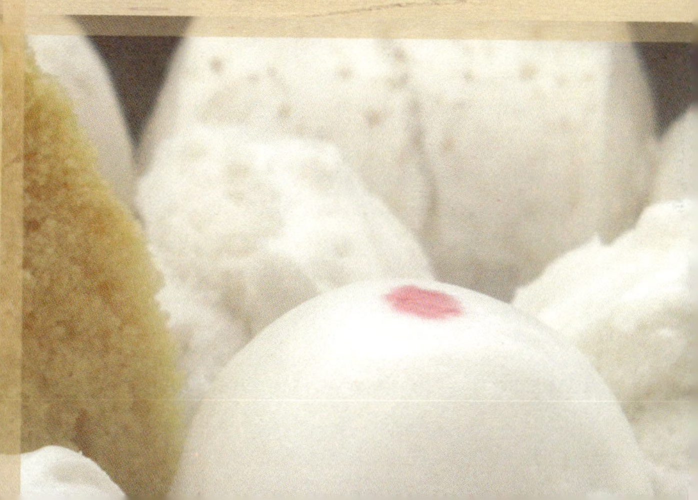

Into the Rain. . .

You can always tell when it's about to pour. It feels like you're living inside a massive balloon filled with humidity so oppressive that all you can do is wonder when it's about to burst. And when it finally does, boy does it feel glorious. The rain falls in sheets, torrential and thunderous, moving so fast you can hardly see the drops; only a moving stream, and sometimes a horizontal one at that.

I came to appreciate this more after moving to Vancouver where the rain is always cold and cuts straight to the bone. In Vancouver, you run from the rain, not into it.

But when the sub-tropical rain falls in Hong Kong, it's an altogether different experience. The city grows quiet, takes a collective exhale and when it's all over, the air feels lighter, brighter, like the city just got a good scrubbing from head to toe.

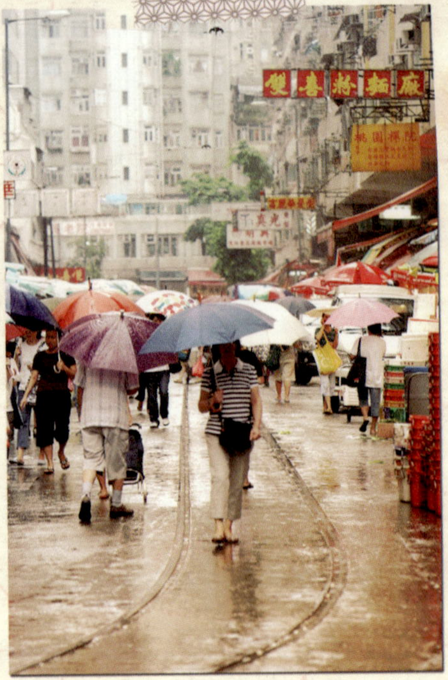

What to do in a deluge: Take a walk through the markets. Ride across the city in a tram. Cosy up to a window and watch the world go by. Try the cafe at the Excelsior Hotel in Causeway Bay (281 Gloucester Rd.), which has views of the harbour and the typhoon shelter. Decades ago, this was where the sampans would huddle during a storm. Today, it's all yachts.

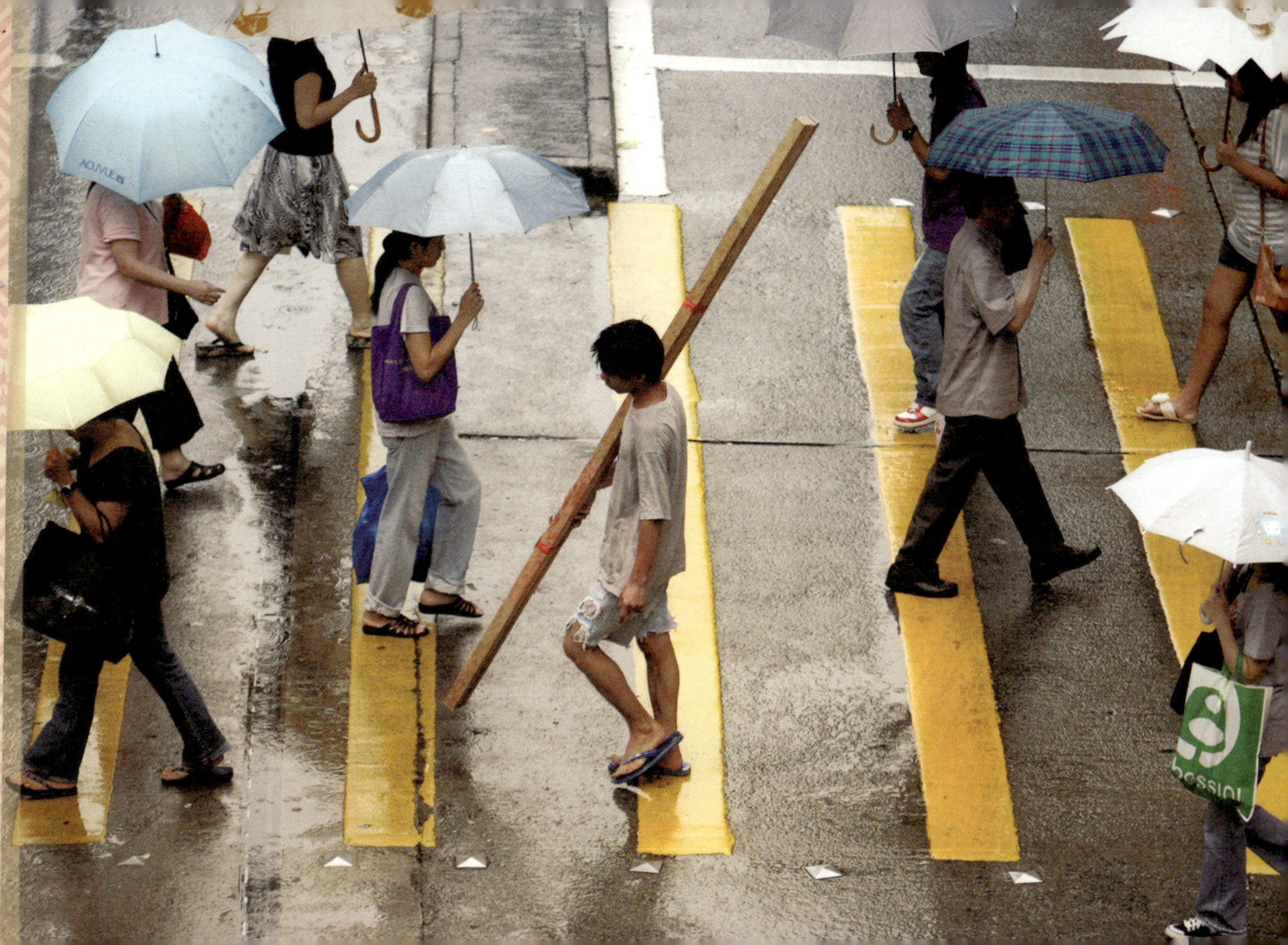
ACUVUE
bossini

Uncle Liu's Gai Dan Jai

Gai dan jai is a deceptively satisfying waffle-y snack every Hong Konger grows up with. Or, as Nick likes to call them: "crispy, chewy, doughy goodness." Uncle Liu, as he's known, sells the city's best gai dan jai. And if our word is not to be believed, then surely the near-constant line outside his shop/stall is evidence enough (not to mention the glowing newspaper and magazine reviews plastered on the exterior walls).

A plump man with a ruddy face and jolly spring to his step, Uncle Liu's mother eked out a living hawking the very same snack years ago. He fondly recalls following her food cart around to various public housing estates "before I was even potty-trained."

As an adult, Uncle Liu followed in his mother's footsteps, first as a street food vendor selling stir-fried sticky rice, then switching to *gai dan jai* about 10 years ago. With just enough funds to lease a tiny commercial space (about large enough for two people), he cut a take-out window in the wall and began cooking aromatic waffle balls, just like his mother did all those years ago.

Uncle Liu

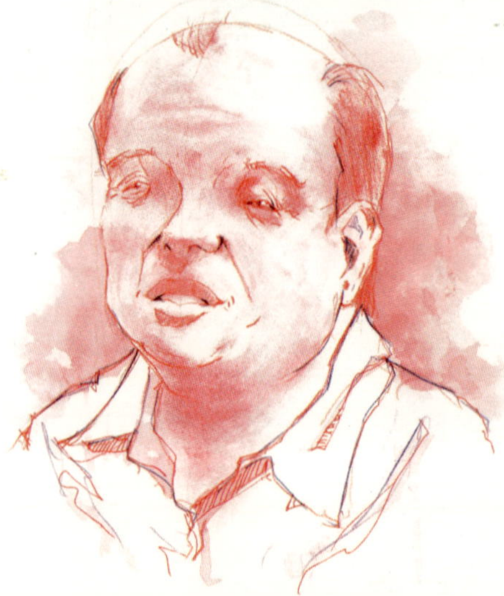

Today, Uncle Liu's *gai dan jai* has attracted a loyal following from celebrities to foodies. Crispy on the outside and light and fluffy on the inside, some customers stop by every day for a little brown bag of waffle balls. So what's the secret? Quite simple, he smiles. "The most important thing is that you put your heart into it."

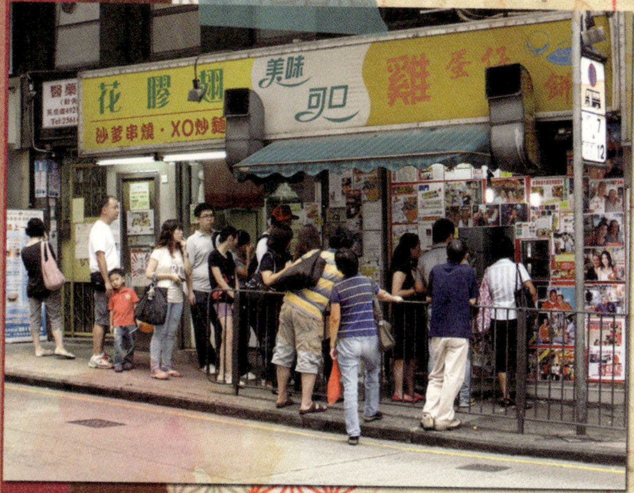

"crispy, chewy, doughy goodness"

- Nick

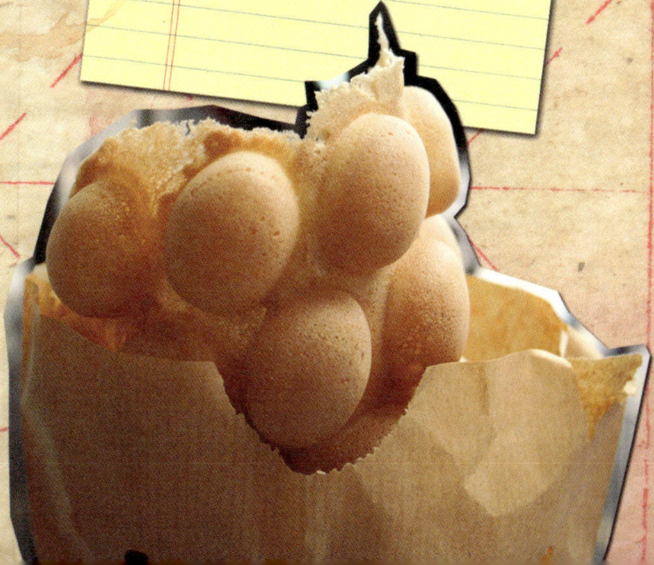

Peers by the Pier

Just as the city begins to stir, the old friends make their way to the pier. They've been doing this for more than a decade, every morning at six on the dot. Some bring newspapers, others bring cigarettes. They head to the railing, where the harbour meets the land, and watch as the ferries chug in from Kowloon.

"We come for conversation. We talk about our family, our country and even tennis-see!" says Dr. Yeung. The dozen or so friends, bonded by history and geography, all hail from Fujian province in southeastern China. Their stories follow a similar script.

Dr. Yeung, a trained surgeon, left mainland China more than 30 years ago to find his future in the south. Hong Kong, then still under British rule, seemed a mecca of opportunity while China remained under the iron-fisted rule of the Chinese Communist Party. His friend, Mr. Wong, puts it more pointedly: "We came for this," he says, his hand gesturing towards his mouth.

But life here had its problems, too. As Dr. Yeung tells it, discrimination against mainlanders made it difficult for him to obtain a medical licence. He had no choice but to

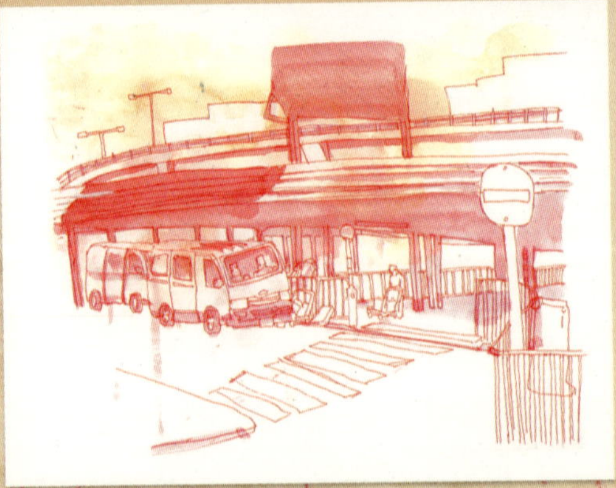

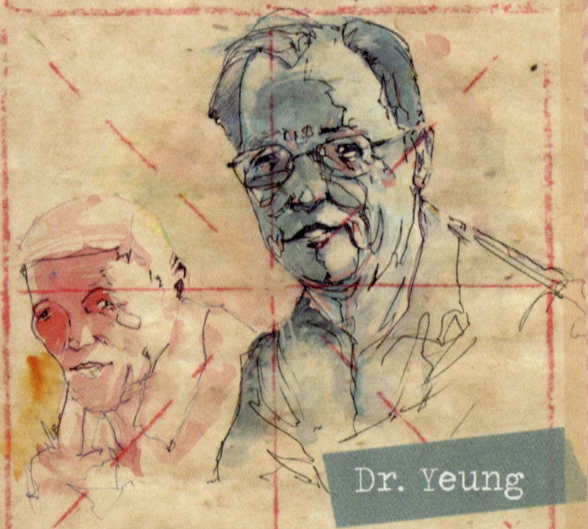

Dr. Yeung

improvise. “I opened a traditional Chinese medicine shop, but used my knowledge of western medicine,” he says proudly.

Despite the hardships, this was clearly a home he relished. In a city famous for its resilience, Dr. Yeung fit right in. “We were so poor, but there was work,” he says. “I loved it here.”

Now retired, Dr. Yeung and his friends gather daily to talk about days gone by and how Hong Kong just isn’t what it used to be. Their list of complaints is long: The crowds, the traffic, the local government that fails to take care of its seniors. Across the border, the home they left more three decades ago is now brimming with opportunity and optimism. So would he go back, to the home he once turned his back on, after all these years?

“Of course!” he says, without skipping a beat.

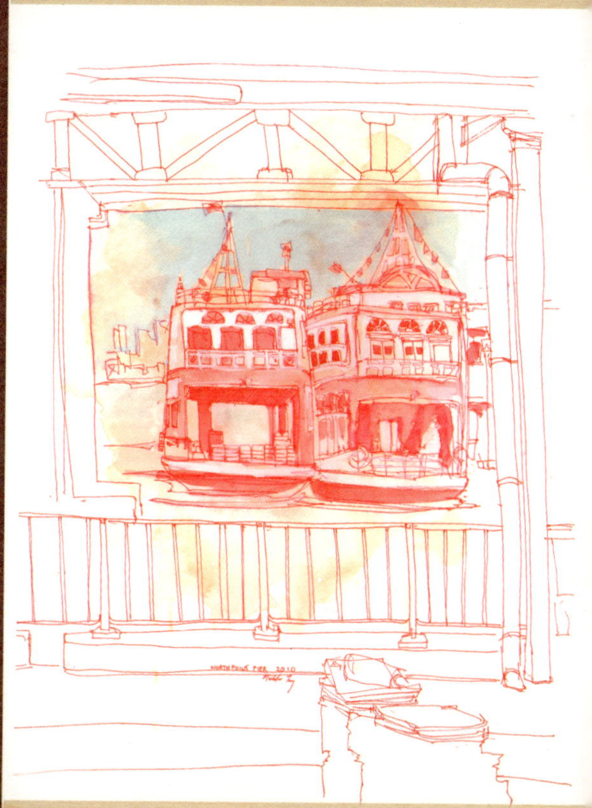

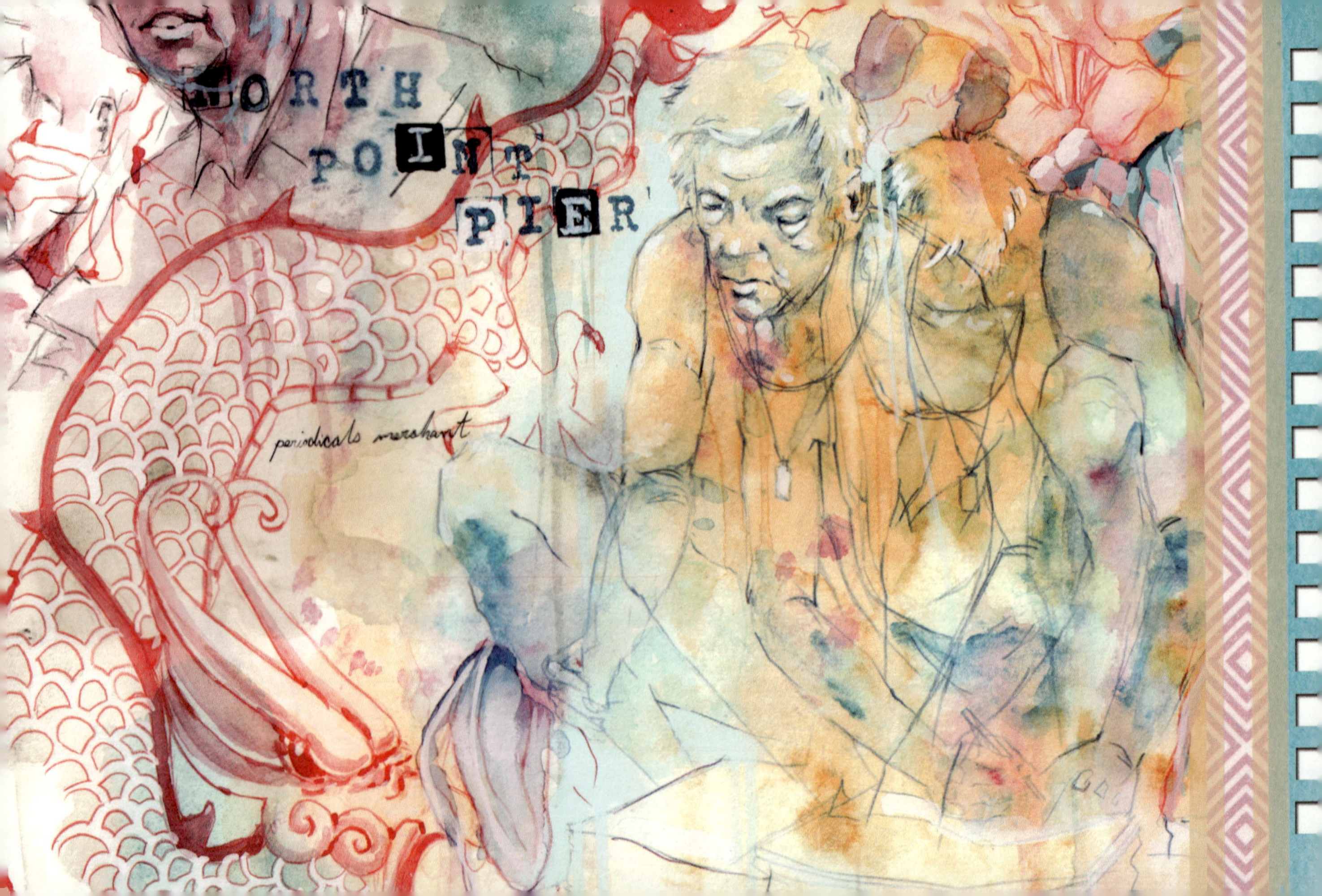
NORTH
POINT
PIER
periodicals merchant

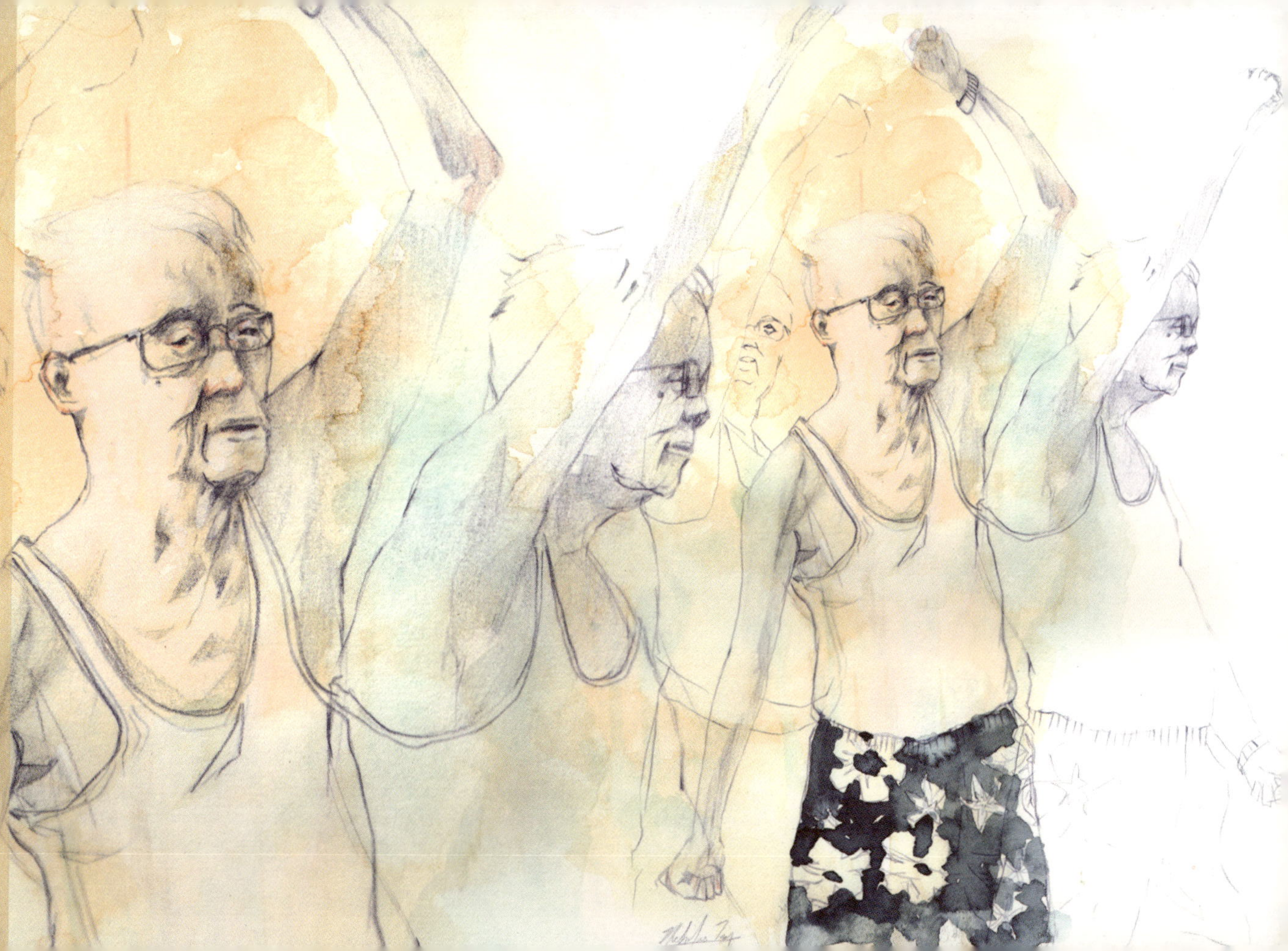

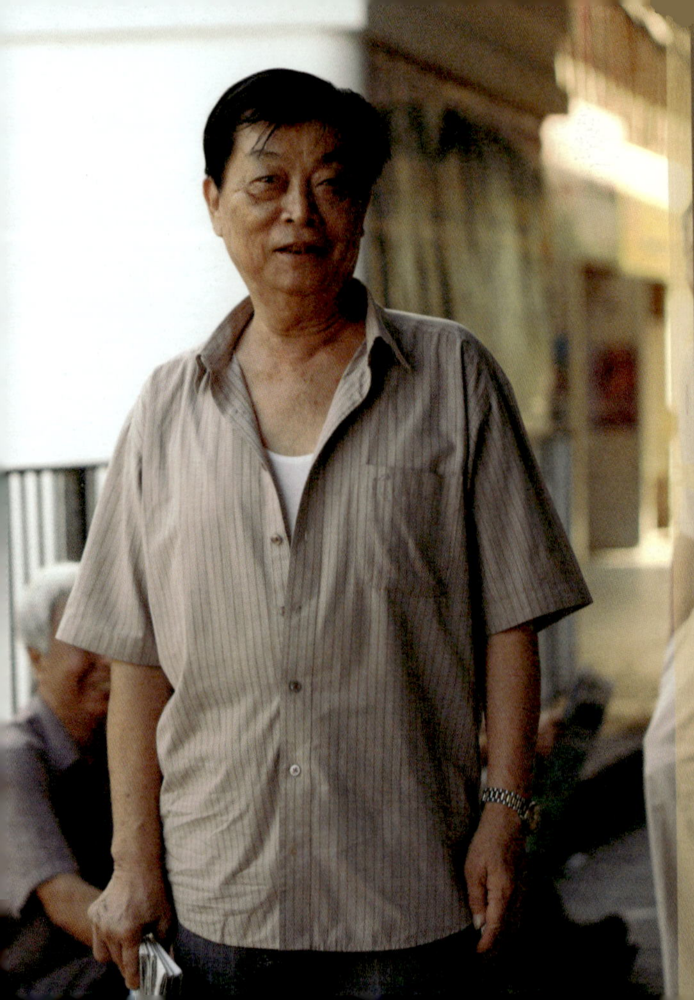

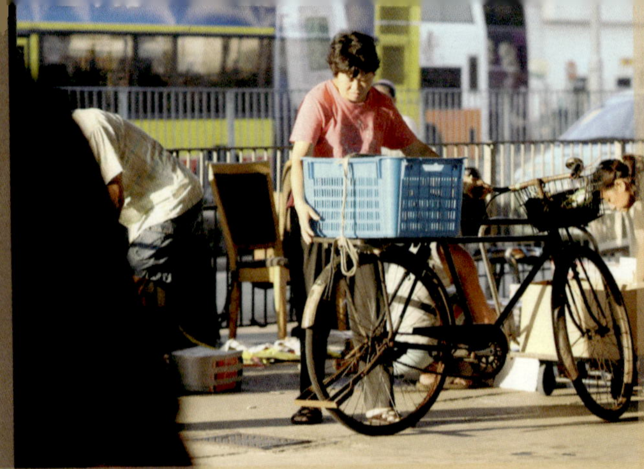

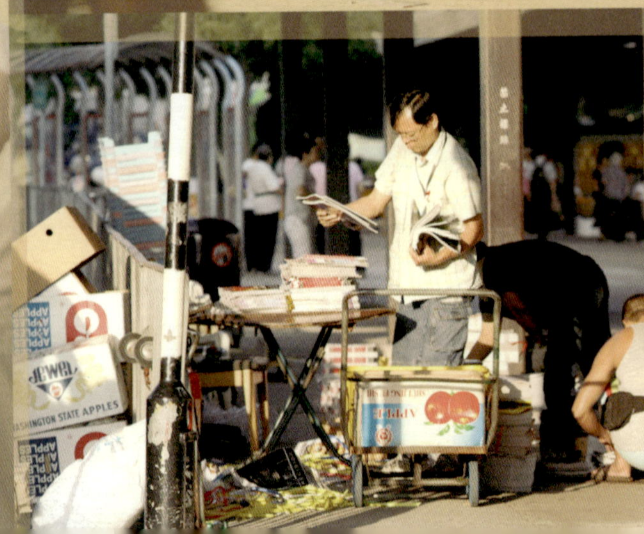

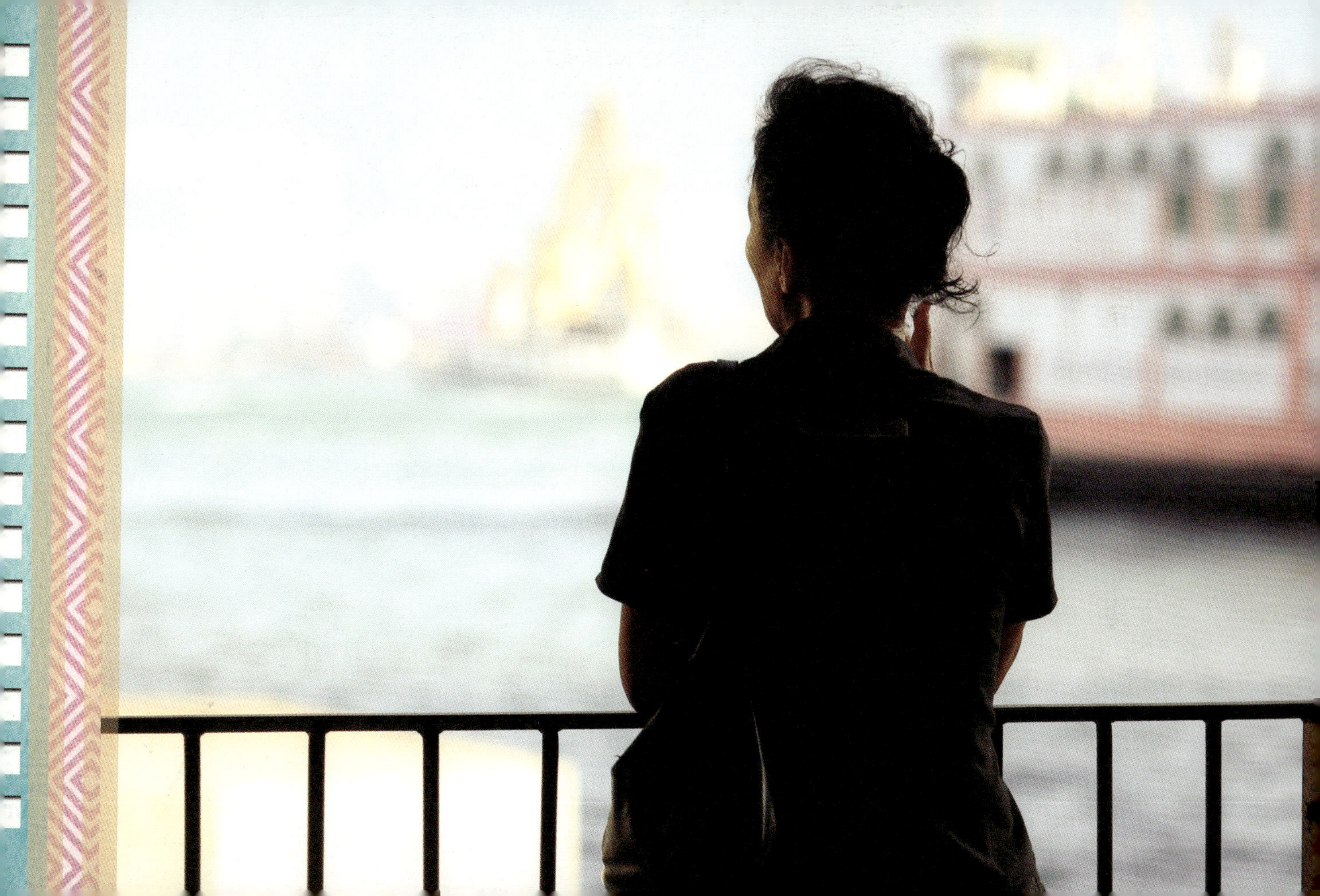

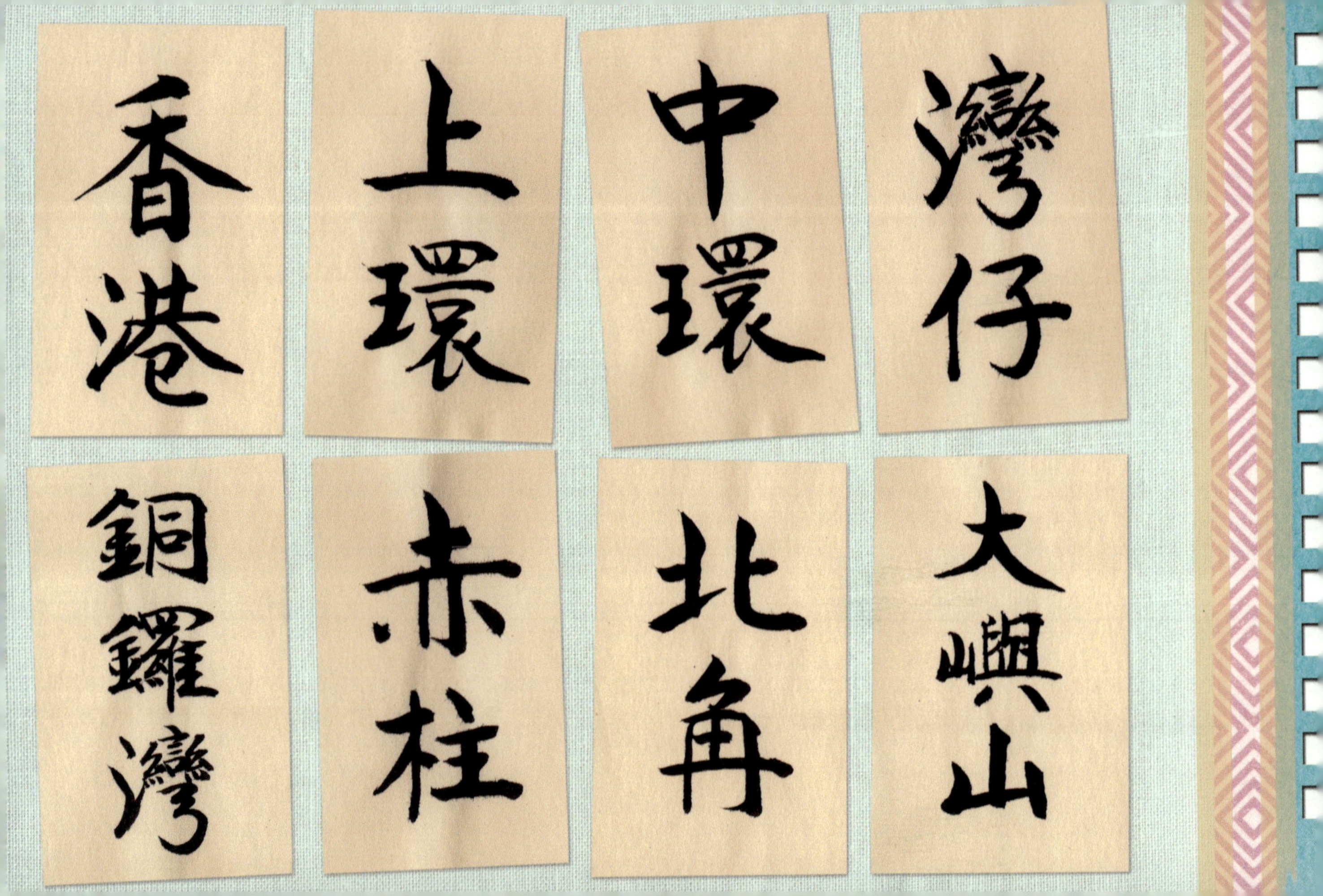
香港
上環
中環
灣仔
銅鑼灣
赤柱
北角
大嶼山

Acknowledgements

Thank you to my husband Nick for gently pushing me in the direction of my dreams and for translating my jumbled thoughts into such a visual delight. I couldn't imagine sharing this beautiful, creative life with anyone else.

To mom and dad for spoiling us at all times, but especially when we are in Hong Kong. And for always having a steaming bowl of *tong* at the ready. To Oz and Tessa for your steadfast belief and optimism.

To my in-laws, *nai nai* and *loh yeh*, for keeping us fed and fuelled as we finished this book whilst in the throes of new parenthood. And to Stimpy for entertaining the little one while we recharged.

To Christina Montgomery for your clear-eyed editor's precision and early guidance. For getting it right from the start, and getting me back up when the going got tough. I am indebted to your support. To Kirk and Kathryn for those early daydreams and coming along with us to explore this city. To Connie for being a girl's best cheerleader. To May and J.C. for opening doors and Pete Spurrier for taking a chance on us.

To our extended circle of family and friends in Hong Kong, this city would not be nearly as fun without you. Thank you for making our visits such a joy. And to everyone who shared with us their slice of Hong Kong, we were fascinated and riveted by your enthusiasm and energy.

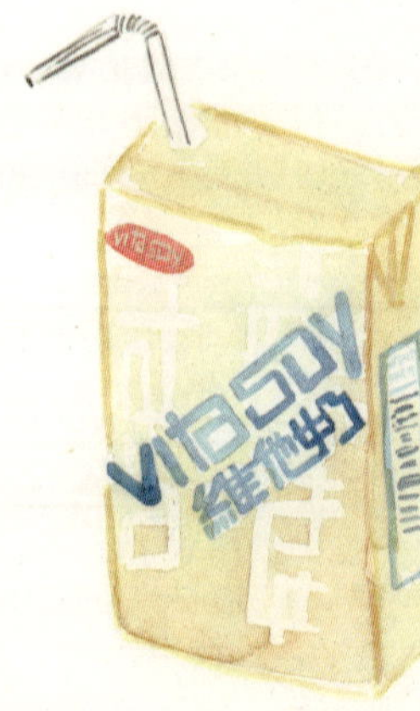
vitasoy
維他奶